The Reformation for Armchair Theologians

Also available in the Armchair Series:

The Reformation for Armchair Theologians

GLENN S. SUNSHINE

ILLUSTRATIONS BY RON HILL

Westminster John Knox Press
LOUISVILLE • LONDON

Book design by Sharon Adams
Cover design by Jennifer K. Cox
Cover illustration by Ron Hill (Left to right: Prince Charles, Frederick the Wise, Henry VIII, Queen Elizabeth, John Knox, Martin Luther, Ulrich Zwingli, and John Calvin).

First edition
Published by Westminster John Knox Press
Louisville, Kentucky

This book is printed on acid-free paper that meets the American National Standards Institute Z39.48 standard. ∞

PRINTED IN THE UNITED STATES OF AMERICA

10 11 12 13 14 — 10 9 8 7 6 5

Library of Congress Cataloging-in-Publication Data

Sunshine, Glenn S.
    The reformation for armchair theologians / Glenn S. Sunshine.— 1st ed.
        p. cm.
    ISBN: 978-0-664-22815-6 (alk. paper)
    1. Reformation. I. Title.

BR305.3.S86 2005
270.6—dc22
                                        2004057201

Contents

Acknowledgments

This book began its life as a series of newsletter articles for First Presbyterian Church in Hartford, Connecticut. These circulated among some other churches before I combined them together and expanded them into the first chapters of this book as part of an adult education class in church history at First Church of Christ in Wethersfield, Connecticut. With the encouragement of readers at these two churches and elsewhere, I decided to complete the project. My thanks to all of you for your support.

On the academic side, I would like to thank Professor John D. Woodbridge of Trinity Evangelical Divinity School, who taught me what it means to be a church historian and whose mantra, "It's not that simple," I have violated consistently throughout this book. I would also like to thank my doctoral advisor, Professor Robert M. Kingdon, now emeritus professor of the University of Wisconsin in Madison, whose classes and seminars shaped much of my understanding of the Reformation and particularly of Calvinism. Neither, of course, is responsible for this text— any errors or omissions are my own—but the work was nonetheless shaped by my opportunity to study with them; I trust they will not be too depressed by the results.

On the technical side, I would like to thank Don McKim, my editor, for his help in moving the project forward, and Ron Hill for the illustrations, which add so much to the volume.

Acknowledgments

On the personal side, I would like to thank my wife Lynn, the love of my life, who read the chapters, put up with the puns, and gave me very sane advice on keeping it understandable. And I would like to dedicate the book to the memory of my father, Nathan Sunshine, and of my father-in-law, Edward Elsner, who would have loved it.

Glenn S. Sunshine
New Britain, Connecticut
February 28, 2004

CHAPTER ONE

On the Eve of the Reformation

The Need for Reform

Before we begin looking at the Reformation proper, we need to back up a bit to the fifteenth century so that we can understand the world out of which Protestantism grew. Luther's ideas did not arise in a vacuum, nor did they catch on and spread without the people of his day being thoroughly primed with the idea that the church needed to be reformed. We will understand the Reformation better if we get to know some of the problems that faced the Catholic Church in the early sixteenth century and look at some of the attempts to clean it up before Luther put reform at the top of nearly everybody's agenda.

The Catholic Church in the fifteenth century was shot through with problems on all levels of the hierarchy. On a local level, parish priests were often completely uneducated, not even understanding the Latin of the Mass that they recited each day. From the perspective of the church, this wasn't really a big problem: Catholic doctrine states that the sacraments operate *ex opere operato,* that is, entirely on the basis of the work of Christ, and thus do not depend on the worthiness or education of the priest; as long as the ritual is performed correctly by a duly ordained priest, the sacrament is valid. And since most of the faithful did not understand Latin either and viewed the priest's work in largely magical terms—the phrase *hocus pocus* is actually a corruption of the Latin *hoc est corpus meum* (this is my body) from the Mass—they did not particularly care about whether or not their local priest was educated either, at least for a while.

But the lack of education among the clergy also meant that basic Christian doctrine was not being communicated to the congregations. The typical parish priest did not even preach regularly; that was left to specialists like the Dominicans, a religious order that was established specifically to preach and whose members traveled from place to place delivering sermons. In cities, finding priests who also preached was less of a problem; urban priests tended to preach more and to be better prepared than their rural counterparts, though in most parts of Europe about 80 percent of the population lived in the countryside. At the same time, the better-educated priests in the towns had to compete with a better-educated laity, particularly after the invention of printing. The results were often rather embarrassing for the priests. For example, in Geneva in 1536, just prior to the city turning Protestant, members of the congregation were known to interrupt preachers, challenging what was said on the basis of the parishioner's own readings in the Bible and shouting the preachers down when they could not respond to the parishioner's satisfaction.

Clerical ignorance was not the only problem the church faced on a local level; concubinage was also quite a problem. Catholic priests were required by canon law (i.e., the laws of the church) to be celibate, but many of them were openly living with women in unofficial common-law style relationships that could not be regularized by marriage. In fact, not only was the practice open, but it was actually welcomed in many cases by both the bishops and the local people. Some bishops encouraged priests to find concubines; since it was illegal, the priests could then be made to pay an annual fine (or if you prefer, a fee) for having the concubine, and the bishop thus had an additional, steady source of income. As far as the locals go, when reform-minded bishops questioned them about their attitudes toward their priest and his concubine, the men often replied that the priest was welcome to his bedwarmer since it made him far less likely to go after their wives and daughters. (Incidentally, monks had an even worse reputation for lechery than local priests did. There was even an entire genre of off-color jokes devoted to immoral monks, more or less like the traveling salesman and farmer's daughter jokes of an earlier generation in America. As far as nuns go, if we are to believe Italian Renaissance writer Giovanni Bocaccio, there were convents in Rome that doubled as brothels. And Luther claimed there were cardinals in the church who were viewed as living saints because they confined their sexual activities to adult women.)

The problems extended well beyond the local level, however. At the episcopal level (i.e., the bishops, the theoretical overseers of the local clergy), there was a wide variety of problems as well. Of course, sexual immorality and ignorance of doctrine and canon law were not confined to the parish priests. Since many bishops were little more than political appointments from prominent families, these kinds of problems extended to the episcopate as well, though their professional staffs could often mitigate at least the worst effects of their lack of education. The more serious problems at this level were corruption, greed, and neglect of the diocese (i.e., the area the bishop was to oversee). The most basic of these was *simony,* named after Simon Magus from Acts 8:9–24. Put simply, simony is the buying and selling of church offices, and it is a crime in canon law. At the same time, however, church leaders (including the pope) used a loophole that enabled them to get around the prohibition, to their own satisfaction at least. Instead of accepting bribes, the popes would make it known that there was a fee for actually assuming the office once selected. The pope could then either set the fee so that only those who could afford it would be candidates for the office, or actually select the highest bidder and set the fee at that level. He would then appoint the candidate, who would give him a kickback in the form of the fee for assuming the office. Closely related to the problem of simony was plurality of offices, that is, a single person holding several offices within the church, including several bishoprics. Again, this was illegal, but with enough financial or political clout a candidate could get a special dispensation to permit him to do this. From this practice flows necessarily a third problem: nonresidence. Whether a multiple office holder or not, some bishops lived outside of their diocese and simply collected the income from it, performing none of their responsibilities and neglecting the churches of their diocese.

The problems with corruption did not stop with the bishops, of course. As we have just seen, the popes themselves were involved in the problems of the episcopacy, and in many ways managed to raise the level of corruption to new heights. The Borgia papacy is probably most notable example of this. The Borgias came from Spain, where the name was Borja. The first of the family to be elected pope was Calixtus III, who held the office from 1455 to 1458. There had been some disagreement over who was to be elected, with the Roman families who had traditionally held a great deal of influence over papal elections splitting seven out of the fifteen cardinals (i.e., officially, priests of the city of Rome who are responsible for electing their bishop; the bishop of Rome is better known as the pope). This enabled the four Spanish cardinals to push their candidate through. Calixtus was old and frail and was expected to be a largely ineffective transitional figure until the politics could sort themselves out. But Calixtus took to the job with real gusto. He worked to suppress the old Roman families so that their power within the Curia (i.e., the papal court) was largely eliminated. Further, while nearly all popes engaged in a certain amount of nepotism (i.e., the appointing of relatives, usually nephews, to positions within the church), Calixtus did it on a grand scale; two nephews were appointed as cardinals, and the cronyism continued literally down to the cooks in the kitchen. One of these nephews who had been made a cardinal, Rodrigo Borgia, was particularly known for partying, having multiple mistresses, and so forth. He had a number of illegitimate children while a cardinal, including Cesare and Lucretia. At the same time, he was an able diplomat, among other things arranging favorable marriages for all of his children. Lucretia's husbands all died rather quickly, a fact which led to her probably undeserved reputation as a poisoner; they may have died of natural causes. (Of course, it has also been suggested that

Cesare murdered them because he was unusually, well, "close" to his sister.) At any rate, in 1492 Rodrigo was elected Pope Alexander VI over his rival Guiliano delle Rovere.

Alexander VI continued the family practice of nepotism, in particular making his illegitimate son Cesare a cardinal. (This was illegal on a number of counts: Cesare wasn't a priest, though of course Rodrigo had not been one either when he had become a cardinal; illegitimacy barred you from becoming a priest, etc. But being pope means you never have to say you're sorry.) Cesare's principal goal was the conquest of the Romagna, also known as the Papal States, a patchwork of largely independent territories nominally under the control of the pope that extended diagonally across the Italian peninsula roughly from Rome to Venice. But Cesare did not want to take over the Romagna for the papacy, its technical overlord; he wanted to do it for the Borgia family. To facilitate this, in 1499 Alexander VI invited the French to invade Italy on the basis of long-standing dynastic claims that the French had to the duchy of Milan (in northern Italy) and the kingdom of Naples (in southern Italy). The details of these claims are pretty confusing; suffice it to say here that this was the second time in recent memory that the French had invaded Italy over them. Alexander VI agreed to support their claims (despite having made a commitment to support Ludovico il Moro Sforza, the current duke of Milan, against rival claimants, including France) in return for French help conquering the Romagna for the Borgias. Cesare, who was a very capable general, dropped the cardinalship and took over the Romagna for his family, becoming a full-fledged Renaissance prince and establishing an autonomous state staffed by Spaniards.

Then in 1503 Alexander VI died. Cesare was violently ill

at the time and couldn't influence the papal election. The cardinals thus elected Pius III, a reform-minded cardinal who opposed many of Alexander's policies. Unfortunately, however, Pius died within a month. Giuliano delle Rovere, Rodrigo Borgia's old rival, was then elected pope, taking the name Julius II. Not surprisingly, Julius made it his goal to get the Romagna back for the papacy and to stick it to the Borgias. He donned armor and led the papal armies personally against Cesare, who was defeated and captured. Cesare was charged with murder, but before he could be brought to trial he broke out of jail. He died (was murdered?) while trying to make a comeback, however. Julius meanwhile took over the Papal States. He kept the administration intact but tied it to the papacy. This was a very expensive process, so he raised funds by openly engaging in simony, as well as selling indulgences (more on that in the next chapter). He was, however, a brilliant if unscrupulous diplomat, a talented administrator, a patron of the arts (e.g., he began the construction of St. Peter's Basilica and was one of Michelangelo's principal patrons), and something of a reformer, notably in banning simony in papal elections and in bringing an end to the practice of nepotism within the papacy.

Though the Borgia papacy is the stuff of opera, and though it is the most extreme example of the type of corruption found among Renaissance popes, it was far from unique. And these examples from the local parish priest to the pope are only the tip of the iceberg. The fact is, the Catholic Church was rife with corruption and thus ripe for reform. This fact was not lost on people of the day; many inside and outside of the church were concerned about the corruption and spiritual malaise they saw around them and suggested programs to try to correct the problems. We turn now to some of these proposals.

Early Reform Proposals

Given the hierarchical nature of the church, it would seem that a systematic reform would have to begin at the top. Unless the pope got his act together, reform of the bishops would be impossible; without the bishops, there was no hope of disciplining the local clergy. But what sort of reform of the papacy was needed? Should the pope get out of temporal politics, power, and wealth altogether? If he didn't spend so much time and effort on these distractions, he would be able to concentrate on his spiritual mission and clean up the church. But if he did this, how could the church defend itself against unscrupulous secular powers? How could the pope enforce his decisions and maintain his authority? Maybe the problem was not that the pope was too wealthy and powerful but that he wasn't powerful enough to enforce church decrees. This forced him to compromise in many areas simply to provide himself with the means he needed to support his legitimate authority within the church and society. If he had more political and financial resources, he would be able to devote himself more fully to the cause of Christ. On the other hand, didn't the church's emphasis on treasures on earth rather than treasures in heaven just lead to more corruption? But there were insurmountable practical problems with attempting to diminish the wealth and political clout of the papacy: entrenched power blocks within the Curia refused to accept anything that would reduce their own wealth, power, and authority, which would inevitably follow papal reform. The net result is that by the late 1400s it had become clear that the popes were not going to lead a general reform of the church, and thus reformers began to look elsewhere.

If a centralized reform was out of the question, what

about trying to clean up some of the problems at lower levels within the church hierarchy, in the religious orders or in individual dioceses? The short answer is that this was attempted in some places and met with some limited success, but a more local version of the interests that blocked systematic reform within the papacy also resisted these reforms. Unreformed monks—many of whom were in positions of authority in the monasteries—obviously were not excited about backing the reformers; without the papacy, it was very difficult to reform the episcopate (remember, even Julius II who worked to eliminate simony in papal elections sold bishoprics); secular politics continued to play a role in episcopal elections; and so on. To be sure, there were some monasteries and dioceses that were reformed, but this fell far short of the systematic efforts needed to root out corruption within the Church as a whole.

If neither episcopal nor papal reform was workable, what about starting with the parish priests? After all, most of the people never dealt with the pope or even bishops; if their priests were better educated, if discipline were enforced (for example, celibacy), this would have the most direct impact on the overall religious climate in the church, perhaps even leading to more systematic reform. But in practical terms, how could you enforce morality among the clergy without the support of the bishops, who, together with at least some of the people, liked the idea of clerical concubinage? How do you convince the bishops to devote resources they are already spending elsewhere to educating their priests? And how do you convince an educated man to accept a position as a priest of a small farming village in the middle of nowhere rather than a more lucrative position in a town or in secular or ecclesiastical administration?

Curiously enough, though none of the church's internal

reform programs proved to be effective, this did not threaten the position of the church in society. There is one very simple reason for this: The church's principal commodity was salvation, and it had a monopoly on it. No matter how corrupt the church was, no matter how much it was criticized, no matter how many reform programs were dreamed up, debated, even implemented, the church itself was fundamentally unassailable since it was the gatekeeper to heaven. Unlike today, people in the fifteenth and sixteenth century lived daily in the presence of death, and so the afterlife was very much on their minds. As long as the church was the only game in town that could offer salvation, its power could not effectively be challenged.

Of course, there were still movements that attempted sweeping changes within the church, though few had long-term success. For example, in the mid- to late-1300s, John Wycliff tried to lead a reform of the church in England based upon a number of nationalistic ideas, including making the Bible available in English, denying any civil jurisdiction for the church, and arguing that the civil

government had the right to take church property when the clergy failed to do their work. Wycliff was condemned as a heretic after his death, and his bones were dug up and burned. His ideas, however, spread to Bohemia, where Jan Hus adapted them for a nationalistic program of church reform aimed at limiting the power of the Germans over the Slavic peoples of the area, and combining this with vernacular liturgy (i.e., liturgy in the common, spoken language) and with giving the laity the cup during the Eucharist, something which was restricted to priests in medieval Europe. Hus caused such a stir that he was summoned under an imperial safe conduct to a church council meeting at Constance; once there, the safe conduct was revoked, and Hus was arrested, tortured, and burned at the stake. His followers in Bohemia erupted in revolt, and peasant armies led by a brilliant Hussite general named Jan Žižka ("One-eyed John") fought an innovative and brilliant campaign that defeated the imperial army as well as crusading armies sent against them. Eventually, the situation simmered down, but not until Hussite armies had terrorized the Holy Roman Empire (see chapter 2) nearly to the Baltic. The Bohemians received some concessions—notably the right to give the cup to the laity during Communion—but there was no long-term impact on the church. The only lasting effect of the whole incident was not religious but political: Fear of the Hussites continued to afflict many parts of the empire for generations to come. Keep that in mind—you'll be seeing it later.

This does not mean, however, that reform programs were complete failures. In fact, two major programs did have quite a bit of success, perhaps because they were primarily focused on the laity rather than the church hierarchy. The first of these was the Brethren of the Common Life, founded in the late fourteenth century by Gerhard Groote in the Netherlands. (Groote's first group was actually the Sisters of the Common Life, but they have been largely and unfortunately forgotten.) The Brethren of the Common Life adopted a lifestyle that was an implicit criticism of the church, while at the same time continuing to attend Mass, to use sympathetic priests as confessors, and so forth. They practiced the *devotio moderna,* or "renewed devotion," an approach to Christianity that focused on developing a close, emotional identification with Christ at key points in his life, especially his passion. This led to a process of "continual conversion" where the practitioner's vices were gradually replaced by virtues. To put that differently, the *devotio moderna* was concerned with changing the believer's heart, the wellspring of behavior, rather than focusing only on external actions. The Brethren had little use for speculative theology, advocating instead contemplative reading of the Bible, communal life, ordered prayer, church attendance, and self-examination. Of necessity, they were also involved in education to give people the skills they needed to read the Bible and other devotional works. In fact, by the sixteenth century, virtually everyone in Germany and the Low Countries who received a basic education got it in schools run by the Brethren of the Common Life.

The second of these reform programs, Renaissance humanism, was focused not so much on religion as on education, though it did have profound implications for religious life as well. In fact, humanism is so important in setting the stage for the Reformation—and so widely misunderstood—that it deserves a section of its own.

Renaissance Humanism

Today the word *humanist* has philosophical overtones, usually denoting someone who emphasizes human autonomy, moral relativism, perhaps atheism, and so on. In the Renaissance, however, the word meant something completely different. A humanist was simply a student of the humanities, a group of subjects that included rhetoric, moral philosophy (i.e., ethics), history, and poetry. Of these, rhetoric—the art of speaking or writing in a clear, convincing style—was the most important. This was an important change from medieval priorities, where education was structured around the seven liberal arts—the trivium (grammar, rhetoric, and logic) and the quadrivium (arithmetic, geometry, astronomy, and music)—with logic as the main focus.

There were several reasons why Renaissance thinkers moved from the liberal arts to the humanities. One of them was practicality; the humanities were seen as far more effective in preparing people to play an active role in society. You don't think the humanities look practical? Compare it to the liberal arts and its emphasis on logic. Have you ever been in a discussion with someone who presented you with an argument that you couldn't find any flaws in, but that somehow didn't convince you? That's the problem with logic: "A man convinced against his will is of the same opinion still." A case can fit all the criteria for logical cogency and still not be convincing. Rhetoric, on the other hand, is designed to convince and to move people to action; it's far more practical. The problem is, teaching rhetoric by itself is like handing someone a loaded gun. Hitler was one of the greatest orators of the twentieth century; his speeches were far more subtle than just the five seconds of ranting and raving we usually see in the Allied propaganda newsreels. And the effect of his oratorical abilities was nine million people dead in the Holocaust. Rhetoric without moral philosophy kills, and thus if you're going to teach rhetoric, you must teach moral philosophy

and instability that characterized his whole life. He was educated in the schools of the Brethren of the Common Life, and then went on to the University of Paris, which he hated and soon left. He was a born scholar, however, and was particularly taken with the writings of the Italian humanists. Under Valla's inspiration, Erasmus set out to become the greatest Latin scholar of his day. His earliest career was as a monk. Although this was supposed to mean he had to live in his monastery, he constantly found excuses to travel so he could advance his studies; he eventually received a dispensation from the pope not to return to the monastery at all. His next career was as a tutor to the rich, including Lord Mountjoy in Paris, which earned him a trip to England, where he became friends with Sir Thomas More and met King Henry VIII. From there he traveled to Italy, where among other things he worked as an assistant to a printer in Venice that specialized in Greek texts. This gave Erasmus the opportunity to perfect his knowledge of

Greek. He spent much of the rest of his life working with printers, either writing original works or preparing editions of classical and early Christian writers. His best-known work today is *The Praise of Folly,* an incredibly funny piece he whipped off in a weekend to amuse himself. My personal favorite is *Julius Exclusus,* a savage, libelous, and very funny satire on the warrior pope Julius II, which discusses what happened when Julius died and tried to get into the pearly gates past a skeptical St. Peter. Ultimately, Erasmus has Julius threaten to assemble his army, which was likely to get slaughtered in battle before long, and blast his way into heaven with his cannons.

Arguably, Erasmus's most important works, however, were those dealing with religion. For example, Erasmus published the first printed text of the Greek New Testament in 1516, together with a fresh Latin translation of the New Testament. This work rankled lots of theologians, who had made their living spinning out elaborate logical deductions on the basis of the specific wordings of the Vulgate, the Latin translation of the Bible that had been in use for the past one thousand years. In addition to his editions of the New Testament and early Christian writers, Erasmus wrote such works as the *Complaint of Peace,* a defense of limited Christian pacifism, the *Handbook of the Militant Christian* (also called the *Enchiridion*), and others that advocated a thorough reform of the church. *Julius Exclusus* fits into this category as well, since it is a spirited attack on papal abuses. In these works, Erasmus promoted a vision of church reform based on scholarship, a return to the Bible and the early church, and an end to abuses. This approach had its roots in the *devotio moderna,* though Erasmus gave it a different spin by extending it beyond personal piety to a comprehensive reform of church institutions based in true humanist fashion on the model of the early church.

Erasmus's ideas won over a significant percentage of the church hierarchy, many of whom by this point were trained humanists themselves. The Erasmian reform program seems to have been on the verge of triggering the long-awaited systematic reform of the church when it was overtaken by events in Germany. Ironically enough, Erasmus's emphasis on reform of practice put him on a collision course with a man whose attempt to correct another abuse of practice in the church would catapult him to the center of a far more sweeping reform than either he or Erasmus had envisioned—a man by the name of Martin Luther.

Questions for Discussion

1. In view of the widespread corruption in the church, why do you think more people didn't just give up on the institution? Is there a difference between their reaction and reactions to problems in the institutional church today? How do you explain these differences or similarities?

2. In the absence of outside competition, is it possible to reform an institution from the inside? Or were the internal reform programs in the late medieval church doomed to fail without the threat posed by churches that did not owe their allegiance to Rome?

3. How were the *devotio moderna* and Renaissance humanism alike? How were they different? How do they compare with ideas on reforming church and society today?

4. Do you think that Erasmus's program of educating priests and cleaning up abusive practices following the model of the early church would have been enough to reform the church? Why or why not?

CHAPTER TWO

Martin Luther and the Break with Rome

Luther's Early Life and Conversion

Martin Luther did not set out to be a reformer; it was a role that he more or less backed into. In fact, Luther did not originally intend to become a churchman at all. Luther's father, Hans, was a mining engineer in Saxony in eastern Germany, then a part of the Holy Roman Empire. Technological changes had expanded silver production throughout this region, and Saxony prospered. Its ruler, Frederick the Wise, had used some of the money he made from silver to establish a new university at his capital city of Wittenberg (1502). Hans Luther had also prospered because of the silver boom, so much so that he was able to send his son Martin to the University of Erfurt, intending for him to become a lawyer. But a sudden, unexpected thunderstorm changed all that.

Martin was traveling home from the university when he was caught by an exceptionally violent storm. In fact, a bolt of lightning struck close enough to Martin that he was thrown off his horse. Convinced he was going to die, he said, "St. Anne, save me! I will become a monk!" (St. Anne was the patron saint of miners; becoming a monk was considered the height of spirituality in the medieval world, so in effect, Luther was trying to bribe God via St. Anne by promising to dedicate his life to God's service if he survived.) Martin did survive the storm, and when he arrived home, he told his father that he had made a vow to become a monk, so he would not be able to enter law school. Hans was furious, but there was nothing he could do about it. Martin entered an Augustinian monastery, where he became a priest. He also studied theology at the University of Erfurt, where he would eventually receive his doctorate (1512). But the most important thing about Luther's career in the monastery had little to do with his external achievements; instead, it had everything to do with an internal struggle over guilt, a struggle whose resolution led to the most important insights into theology of Luther's entire career.

When Luther entered the monastery, he thought it would please God and contribute to his salvation. And for a while Luther seems to have been a pretty normal monk. Soon, though, he began having severe problems with guilt, problems that bordered on psychosis. According to theologian R. C. Sproul, the issue that faced Luther came from legal reasoning on Jesus's words in the Gospel. When asked what the greatest commandment was, Jesus replied, "Love the Lord your God with all your heart, soul, mind, and strength," in short, with every fiber of your being. So

Luther asked himself, "What is the greatest sin?" The only possible answer was, "*Not* loving the Lord with your whole heart, soul, mind, and strength." When Luther examined himself by this standard, he realized that his emotions, his will, his thoughts and actions were not controlled by love of God, and thus they were all violations of the greatest commandment and mortal sins. The net result was that Luther became increasingly frantic about his guilt, spending hours every day in confession to his spiritual director and nearly driving the poor man to distraction as Luther ransacked his brain and confessed every possible thought and deed from his entire life that could be considered a sin. Finally, in exasperation, his confessor told Luther to go away and only come back when he had something real to confess. Still, Luther found no relief. He engaged in more and more extreme penitential practices to punish himself for his sins, but he still felt unforgiven. He went on a pilgrimage to Rome as part of a delegation from his monastery and engaged in a number of peculiar devotional practices there that were believed to confer grace, but still he was mired in overwhelming feelings of guilt (as well as being disturbed by the corruption he saw in Rome). In short, Luther was in a serious downward slide that very nearly drove him over the edge of sanity.

Then something happened. While in a tower room in the monastery meditating on the Letter to the Romans, Luther was struck by a new interpretation of the phrase "the righteousness of God." Martin had always thought that this phrase referred to God's absolute standards of righteousness that he expected us to live up to. Suddenly it dawned on Martin that the phrase actually referred to righteousness that comes from God to us by faith. Forgiveness of sins and salvation are thus freely available regardless of personal merit or lack thereof; it is all grace operating through faith. This doctrine, known as justification by faith, became one of the hallmarks of Protestantism and one of the few points on which virtually all Protestants agreed. With this "Tower Experience," Luther's guilt melted away and he found himself free. This was Luther's conversion, his experience of being "born again," and was the foundation of everything he would do in his career as a reformer.

The Tower Experience did not lead Luther to reject Catholicism. He believed himself to be well within the bounds of Catholic theology, and it would be some years before the logic of his position, combined with ecclesiastical power politics, would push him to break with Rome, a break he neither intended nor wanted.

Meanwhile, in Italy . . .

To understand the events leading to this break, we must travel south to Rome, where Pope Leo X was building St. Peter's Basilica. Like any of us faced with financing new construction, Leo approached his bankers for a loan. The Medici bank of Florence, which was owned by Leo's family, had been the papal bank for some time, though by Leo's day it had been replaced by the Fugger bank, centered in Augsburg, Germany. The Fugger bank had been founded relatively recently, but it rose rapidly to become the largest bank in the world due to the same silver boom in Germany that had led to the establishment of the University of Wittenberg and the relative prosperity of the Luther family. Jacob Fugger, the head of the bank, approved the loan, but this left Leo with the problem of figuring out how to pay it back. Leo decided that the best approach to handling that problem was to sell off some of the assets in his treasury, specifically, the treasury of merits, of which he was the custodian. In other words, Leo decided to hold an indulgence sale.

What are indulgences? To understand that, we need to know something about Roman Catholic conceptions of sin. According to Catholic theology, every sin you commit results in both eternal and temporal penalties. Eternal penalties affect your relationship with God; they are spiritual and deal with your status in eternity, that is, whether you go to heaven or hell. But since a sin against God is also a crime against your neighbor, sins must also be punished in this life; hence the temporal penalties, which are paid in time. When you confess your sins to a priest and he absolves you, that absolution takes away the eternal penalty due to your sins but leaves the temporal untouched. He then assigns you a penance (a good work) that you can perform that pays the temporal penalty. This may be saying prayers, going on a pilgrimage, and so forth. These penalties could be pretty hefty; for example, each knight who fought at the Battle of Hastings in 1066, in a campaign that had been blessed by the pope, was required to do ten years of penance for every person he killed in the battle. And this didn't even touch other battles the knight fought in or any extracurricular activities he might have indulged in. If you die with your temporal debt unpaid, the remainder has to be paid in time in the afterlife, so you go to purgatory, a doctrine developed in the twelfth century to deal with the problems associated with unpaid temporal penalties. After your temporal penalty is completely paid in purgatory, then you go to heaven.

So how do you avoid languishing in purgatory for who knows how long? There are a couple of possibilities. You could endow a monastery or a church and get priests to say Mass or monks to pray for you. If you pay the expenses, the credit for the time and the Masses goes to your account.

This may seem odd, but think of it like this: If you get a speeding ticket, the town doesn't really care if you pay it or someone else does; it just wants its money. The same logic applies here. As long as your temporal debt is paid by someone, it counts. Going on a pilgrimage is another good option. Not only do you get credit for the time you spend on the road, but the shrine you're visiting itself conveys a certain number of years of penance depending on its importance.

This is where indulgences came in, particularly in connection with armed, fighting pilgrimages, or as we call them, Crusades. To try to drum up troops to free the Holy Land, the pope had promised certain unspecified spiritual benefits to all who fought for the faith; the church then needed to figure out exactly what these benefits were. The doctrines outlined above were elaborated to a large extent to answer this question. The church eventually decided that going on a Crusade would remit the entire temporal penalty due to sins that had been confessed to a priest and absolved. But since not everyone could go on a Crusade—women, the sick, the aged—and not everyone who wanted to go on Crusade could afford it, it was decided that if you paid the way for someone else to go on a Crusade, you would receive the benefits of crusading yourself. These benefits would be paid to you out of the treasury of merits, the collection of good works performed by Christ and the saints above and beyond what was necessary for their own salvation. The pope was the custodian of this treasury and could call a Crusade and authorize a withdrawal for the participants. (Not all the Crusades were to the Holy Land; the *Reconquistà*, which drove the Muslims out of Spain actually began before the Crusades proper, and other Crusades were called against the Albigensians in France, pagans in the Baltic, the Hussites in Bohemia, and even the pope's political rivals.) With the end of the Crusades, the practice of selling indulgences, as these crusading benefits were called, continued. Some were limited indulgences, which paid only for a specific period of time, say, ten years of penance. Others were plenary indulgences, which paid the whole penalty. Leo's indulgence sale was the latter type.

Leo, of course, was not going to go out hawking indulgences on the streets. The man who was reputed to have said, "God gave us the papacy; let us enjoy it!" was not about to turn himself into a salesman. Instead, he let it be known that for a fee, he would authorize other ecclesiastical authorities to sell plenary indulgences themselves. One person who bought into the scheme was Archbishop Albrecht of Mainz, in the Holy Roman Empire. Albrecht wasn't about to peddle indulgences on the corner any more than the pope was, so he subcontracted the indulgences sale to the Dominicans, an order of friars founded in the thirteenth century to supply the church with preachers and expert theologians. The Dominicans would sell the indulgences and take a cut of the profits; the rest would go to Albrecht to recoup the money he had paid Leo to hold the indulgence sale; Leo used Albrecht's money to help pay back the loan he had gotten from the Fugger bank to build St. Peter's Basilica.

Unfortunately, the Dominicans were not above twisting the theology of indulgences to make more sales. One of them, Johan Tetzel, was a master of the hard sell and was generally the sort of person who would give used car salesmen a bad name. He literally would tell his listeners that his indulgences were so good that even if you had violated the Blessed Virgin Mary herself, this would get you off the hook. He told people repentance wasn't necessary for the indulgences to work and that they were a virtual ticket to heaven regardless of what you had done or would do. And when he couldn't get any more sales from that, he ratcheted things up a bit more. If you are not worried about yourself, what about your dearly departed mother languishing perhaps for thousands of years in purgatory? Were you to spend but a few coins on an indulgence, she would be released to go directly into heaven. After going on about this for a while, Tetzel would end with a little jingle: "As soon as the coin in the coin box rings, another soul from purgatory springs!" (It rhymes in German too.) There was no mention that indulgences applied only to sins already committed, confessed to a priest and absolved, only to the temporal penalties due to such sins, and so forth.

The Indulgence Controversy and the Ninety-five Theses

This indulgence sale upset many people. Among them was Elector Frederick the Wise, the prince of Electoral Saxony and one of the people who elected the Holy Roman Emperor. He opposed the indulgence sale for two basic reasons. First, it meant that money his people were producing in Saxony was being sent out of the country to Mainz and ultimately to Rome, thereby hurting the prosperity of Electoral Saxony. In fact, Frederick suspected the whole thing was a scam designed to enrich Italy at the expense of Germany. Second, in addition to using his revenues from silver mining to build the University of Wittenberg, he had also spent a great deal of it purchasing relics; in fact, he had one of the largest relic collections ever assembled. People went on pilgrimages to view these relics—further enriching Saxony's coffers—and Frederick was afraid that the indulgence sale would hurt business. So Frederick simply banned the Dominicans from his territories; Tetzel and company were forbidden to set foot in Sax-

ony, and thus the indulgence sale had none of the negative consequences that Frederick feared.

This wasn't the end of the matter, however. The University of Wittenberg had picked up a star theologian from the University of Erfurt, an Augustinian monk by the name of Martin Luther. He had begun work as a bachelor lecturer at Wittenberg, then completed his doctorate in theology a few years later. Luther was very proud of that doctorate, and always referred to himself as "Herr Dr. Luther." Luther had a new approach to theology based on the insights he gained from his Tower Experience; he and his students had converted the rest of the theological faculty at Wittenberg to his way of thinking. And, like Frederick, Luther was also upset about the indulgence sale, though more for theological reasons, and thus he decided to back up his prince by doing what theologians did in the sixteenth century: He challenged the Dominicans to a debate. Debates were the standard academic exercise of the period, more or less like a combination of term papers and exams today. The protocol involved first writing a list of propositions, or theses, in Latin (the language of academia), which the debater was willing to defend against either specified individuals or all comers. He then posted the theses along with information on the time and place of the debate on the university bulletin board. In theological debates, the theses also had to be sent to the person's spiritual superior to be checked for heresy. Luther wrote a series of theses against the abuses of this indulgence sale— ninety-five of them, to be exact—and posted them on the university bulletin board, the church door at Wittenberg. This has often been portrayed as a great act of defiance, as Luther boldly challenging the corruption of the church. Actually, it was more like an act of conformity. All Luther was doing was following standard procedures for debate in an attempt to defend what he thought was good church doctrine against the abuses of the Dominicans. Although the debate never took place (remember, the Dominicans couldn't enter Saxony), two things came together to make the Ninety-five Theses an enormously controversial event.

First, following standard procedures, Luther sent a copy of the theses to his spiritual superior, who happened to be Archbishop Albrecht of Mainz. Like Queen Victoria, he was "not amused." Second, some of Luther's students got hold of the theses, thought, "This is really hot stuff," and sent them off to a printer *after translating them into German*. Much to everyone's surprise, the Ninety-five Theses became a runaway best seller, with translations following into most European languages. Despite the best efforts of professors since then, this was the only time in history that an academic exercise has generated such an incredible volume of sales. Luther thus unexpectedly found himself at the center of an international controversy over indulgences.

The reason the controversy grew so heated and generated so much interest was that the issues Luther raised went far beyond the details of a particular indulgence sale. Although initially about indulgences, the theological scope of the controversy rapidly expanded. Luther may have been trying to defend good Catholic doctrine against the abuse of the Dominicans, but the way he went about doing this implicitly attacked much of the generally accepted theology of the Catholic Church. Soon questions about indulgences were overshadowed by issues of free will and divine grace, and by the most basic questions of religious authority: How do you settle theological questions? Where do you go to get answers?

The Leipzig Debate (1519)

The controversy got so acrimonious that one of the territorial rulers within the empire, Duke George of Ducal Saxony (not the same as Electoral Saxony, where Luther lived), called a debate in Leipzig in 1519 to try to settle the quarrel. Luther's side was represented by Andreas Karlstadt, one of the other theology professors at Wittenberg with Luther. Karlstadt was chosen for two reasons: first, to show that the ideas did not represent simply Luther's private opinion but had been adopted by the entire theological faculty at Wittenberg; second, Karlstadt was a better speaker (though not a better debater) than Luther. The opposing side was represented by Johann Eck, a theologian from Ingolstadt. Eck, who would make a career of attacking Luther and his ideas, was an absolutely first-class debater; he quickly got the better of Karlstadt, who was then pulled out and replaced by Luther.

A quick note about sixteenth-century debate. These days, when we think of debates, we generally think of something rather formal and controlled with a set form of presentations and rebuttals. While some of this structure was the same in the sixteenth century, debates in this period tended to be a lot wilder and woollier than their

modern counterparts, with cheap shots, *ad hominem* attacks, insults, innuendo, slander, and the like being a normal part of the proceedings. Case in point: Luther habitually referred to Herr Dr. Eck as if the *Dr.* were part of his name, as *Herr Dreck. Dreck* is the German word for "dirt," though dirt of a very specific kind. You can have chicken dirt, cow dirt, horse dirt. . . . Eck returned the compliment by referring to Luther as *Herr Lügner,* "Mr. Liar," omitting the *Dr.* along the way.

Along with this kind of thing, substantive issues were also discussed. In general, Luther held his own, though he did get blindsided when Eck accused him of being a Hussite. This was a shrewd move, because the Hussites were not only heretics, but their armies had struck real fear in the hearts of people in this part of Germany. Associating Luther with Hus would, Eck hoped, turn the crowd against Luther. Further, Eck had a point: Many of Luther's ideas were anticipated by Hus, though Luther himself didn't realize this. In any event, Luther indignantly rejected the charge, so Eck supplied Luther with a few of Hus's books to read. The next day, Eck asked Luther if he still denied that he was a Hussite. Luther responded, no, he was in fact a Hussite, but that simply proved his point: The church should never have condemned Hus, and that demonstrated that even ecumenical councils can and did make mistakes. And so it went. We will deal with the theological issues in the next chapter; suffice it to say here that no immediate decision was made on the winner of the debate. Instead, transcripts of the debate were sent to the Universities of Erfurt (Luther's alma mater) and Paris (the most prominent theological school in Europe). Erfurt refused to decide the case; the issues involved were simply too thorny. Paris stalled. Meanwhile, two other universities decided to get into the act. Louvain, a university with close ties to the papacy, and Cologne, a Dominican school, both condemned Luther.

In the meantime, Luther was rethinking his position. Eck had pushed Luther to greater and greater consistency with his own statements at the Leipzig Debate, and now Luther needed to reevaluate his theological views. It had been made abundantly clear to him that his ideas no longer fit in with Catholic theology, however much he had thought that they did. But, as they say in Wisconsin, "You can always tell a German, but you can't tell him much." Luther was not about to back off from his ideas, so instead he went on the attack. Between 1519 and 1520, Luther published six major treatises attacking Catholic doctrine on a wide range of fronts: forgiveness of sins, grace, free will, the sacraments, the papacy, and so forth. The University of Paris then condemned Luther on the basis of these rather than the transcripts from Leipzig. Pope Leo X, who initially dismissed the controversy as "a monks' quarrel," a turf war between Luther's Augustinians and Tetzel's Dominicans, finally woke up and realized that things were getting out of hand, so he issued a blanket condemnation of everything Luther had ever written and gave him sixty days to recant. Luther refused and so was excommunicated. Luther had enough friends and supporters in high places that he could ignore the excommunication; in fact, he publicly burned it when it arrived. But what Luther could not afford to ignore was that the Holy Roman Emperor decided to become involved in the case as well.

The Diet of Worms (1521): Here I Stand

Before continuing on with Luther's story, it would be a good idea to explain a few things about the Holy Roman Empire. As Voltaire commented, the Holy Roman Empire was a triple misnomer; it was not holy, did not include Rome, and was not an empire. Instead, it was a confederation of states in modern-day Germany, Austria, the Czech Republic, Slovakia, and parts of Poland and Hungary. The heads of seven of these states elected an emperor to act essentially as a CEO over the whole conglomeration. The last emperor had died in 1519—a lucky time, from Luther's perspective, since the candidates for emperor were too busy fighting among themselves to pay much attention to the religious controversy he had started. These included three powerful, dynamic young kings: Henry VIII (Tudor) of England, Francis I (Valois) of France, and Charles I (Habsburg) of Spain; Elector Frederick was mentioned as a possible candidate as well, but he declined. Henry VIII also dropped out quickly, but Francis and Charles battled it out, each trying to out-bribe the other in an attempt to "inspire" the electors to vote for him. In the end, Charles won by borrowing huge amounts of money from the Fugger bank to pay for votes. So Charles I of Spain became Charles V, Holy Roman Emperor, in 1519. After spending nearly two years moving and setting up his government, Charles was able to turn his attention to the religious chaos that was tearing the empire apart. No ruler in the sixteenth century believed that it was possible or desirable to separate religion and politics. And like all Habsburgs, Charles was a loyal Catholic, though like all Holy Roman Emperors, he did not care for the pope, who was his main rival for the status of leader of the Christian world.

In 1521, Charles summoned Luther to appear before him at the Diet of Worms. I know you're waiting with baited breath to find out what that is, so here goes: The Imperial Diet, or *Reichstag,* was the empire's legislative body, like England's Parliament. It was tricameral, with one house for the seven electors, one for the other territorial states, and one for the Imperial Free Cities, a group of towns that were directly under the authority of the emperor rather than under one of the states within the empire. The Diet rotated through these cities, and this time it was due to meet at Worms. Because Luther had been excommunicated, it was hazardous for him to leave the protection of Elector Frederick, so to encourage him to come, Charles gave Luther a safe conduct to attend the Diet. Unfortunately, however, this was exactly what Hus had when he went to Constance, where the safe conduct was revoked and he met a decidedly unpleasant end. And as Eck had so kindly pointed out, Luther's views were remarkably similar to Hus's. Despite this precedent, Luther decided he needed to take the risk and obey the summons. He went to the Diet, all bluster and bravado about how he was going to confront his opponents and make fools of them. When he arrived, however, he was not given the chance to make his defense; the emperor and the papal legate demanded that he recant and was told to give them a simple yes or no answer. Luther asked for some time to think about it, and he was given the night.

After all his bluster and bravado this might come as a surprise, but Luther was genuinely troubled by one of the arguments presented to him. If Luther was right, did that mean that for a thousand years or more God had abandoned his church, his people, his bride to deception and error? Was it really possible that Luther was pretty much the only person in a thousand years to get it right, to really understand the gospel? Wasn't it more likely that he was mistaken rather than that the whole church, to whom Christ had promised to send the Holy Spirit to guide it into all truth, had utterly missed the point of Christianity? This argument stopped Luther in his tracks and forced him to do some very serious soul searching. When the time came for him to give his reply, he started in on a formal speech but was cut off with a demand that he simply say whether he would recant or not. Luther replied:

> Since then your serene Majesty and your lordships seek a simple answer, I will give it in this manner, neither horned nor toothed. Unless I am convinced by the testimony of the Scriptures or by clear reason (for I do not trust either in the Pope or in councils alone, since it is well known that they have often erred and contradicted themselves), I am bound by the Scriptures I have quoted and my conscience is captive to the Word of God. I cannot and will not retract anything, since it is neither safe nor right to go against

conscience. Here I stand. I cannot do otherwise. May God help me. Amen.

This statement has again often been portrayed as a tremendous act of defiance on the part of Luther, a thundering, fearless, denunciation of the church. But it wasn't. It only came as a result of serious struggle, doubt, uncertainty, and with that, fear of death by fire despite his safe conduct. Fearless this speech was not. But it was genuinely courageous, because courage is only courage when one acts not in the absence of fear, but despite it. Understanding what was really going on here, cutting through the nonsense of the biographers who make Luther into a Christian superhero, doesn't lessen his stature as a leader, but heightens it. He acted with real courage and heroism, and he should be honored for that.

Luther didn't die at Worms; Charles was good to his word, and Luther was permitted to return to Wittenberg. But as soon as he left Worms, Luther was declared an imperial outlaw, making it open season on him. Before he made it back to Wittenberg, his party was beset by a group of armed and masked horsemen, who snatched Luther and led him away. They were agents of Elector Frederick, Luther's patron, who, fearing for the life of his most famous subject, seized him secretly and hid him away at the Wartburg castle. Luther remained there in hiding, directing the reform from a distance, writing, and translating the Bible into German.

Questions for Discussion

1. How would Luther's problems with guilt be dealt with today? Do you think he would have had the room to come to his theological insights in today's climate?

How do you balance the legitimate need for therapy with openness to the work of the Spirit?

2. Why do you think the Ninety-five Theses were so popular? How does the condition of the Catholic Church of the day help explain the impact of the Ninety-five Theses on the general public?

3. Given the results of the Ninety-five Theses, do you find it surprising that Luther seems not to have been aware of the distance between his views and the doctrine of the Catholic Church? Why or why not?

4. Why do you think the historical argument about the continuity of the gospel in the church shook Luther up so much? Is this an argument that would have as much impact in today's society? Why or why not?

CHAPTER THREE

Reform of Word and Sacrament

With Luther safely tucked away in the Wartburg castle, we can turn our attention to the issues involved in his conflict with Rome. Luther saw what he was doing as a reform of Word and Sacrament, in other words, of the teaching and essential rituals of the church. The reform of Word breaks down into two broad categories: soteriology (the branch of theology that studies salvation), and authority (where you go to find answers to religious questions). Reform of sacrament flows from the reform of Word and involves the practices that marked out the entire cycle of human life, from birth to death, at least according to Catholic thought. We will survey these issues in this chapter.

Saving Grace

To understand Luther's ideas about salvation, we must first look at late medieval Catholicism's views on the subject. Catholic theologians held a number of competing notions about how one gets to heaven. Mystical theologians, such as Johannes Tauler, argued that within each of us was a divine spark that we had to fan into flames of love to obtain salvation. Among academic theologians, or scholastics, there were two main views. The realist position, held by the Dominicans and promoted by their major theologian Thomas Aquinas, argued that we receive grace at baptism and then must morally cooperate with that grace; our cooperation earns us more grace, and our continued cooperation with that grace earns us salvation as a reward for our efforts. The nominalist position, held by the Franciscans and their theologians such as William Ockham, argued that we begin the process of salvation through our own moral effort; God rewards this effort with grace, which makes possible more moral effort, which again earns us salvation as a reward. Luther was trained in nominalist theology in the University of Erfurt and had read Tauler, so he was well aware of at least these two options. His experience in the monastery, however, led him to reject them categorically.

Luther had been an exemplary monk. After giving up a potentially lucrative career as a lawyer to enter the monastery, he devoted his life to moral effort and to trying to fan the flames of divine love in his life. He was actively engaged in every devotional practice possible, together with regular celebration of the sacraments. Yet he found no peace in them. It was only when he came upon the idea that we are saved exclusively by God's grace which comes to us entirely by faith that his problems with guilt were resolved. Luther argued that Christ's death on the cross, his resurrection, and his ascension to heaven provided everything that we need for our sins to be forgiven; to argue that we contribute anything to our own salvation is close to blasphemy, since it says that we can by our own effort add to the work of Christ. We can only obtain forgiveness of sins on the basis of Christ's work, which is applied to us by God's undeserved mercy as a gift of grace coming to us through faith. Given this, Luther argued that all of the Catholic ideas about soteriology were fatally flawed. He rejected Tauler's mystical theology because his notion of a divine spark within us denied that all of our faculties are corrupt and subject to the effects of sin (a doctrine known as *original sin*). Further, Tauler placed the burden of salvation on us, taking away from the all-sufficient work of Christ. Besides, according to the apostle Paul, we are saved by faith, not love, so Tauler was barking up the wrong tree anyway. Luther also rejected the nominalist idea that our moral efforts begin the process of salvation; this again denied original sin and resurrected the ancient heresy of Pelagianism (named after Pelagius, a fifth-century British monk who argued that we earn our salvation by our own efforts). When Cardinal Cajetan, a Dominican theologian and one of Luther's earliest opponents, pointed out that Luther's complaints about nominalism didn't apply to the realist position of Thomas Aquinas, Luther promptly stated that the realist position wasn't much better. Though it acknowledged the necessity of grace in beginning the process of salvation, it still required human effort to earn our way into heaven; this made it semi-Pelagianism and still a heresy.

Luther's theology thus developed in part from his biblical studies, as we saw in the last chapter, but also from a reaction against both the Catholic theology of his·day and

39

his personal experience in the monastery. His ideas about the process of salvation were distilled into two Latin phrases. The first was *sola gratia*—we are saved by "grace alone." Since Catholic theology could generally agree with this, with the understanding that grace comes through the sacraments or our good works, Protestants added *sola fide*, that is, saving grace comes to us through "faith alone," not through our works or the sacraments. (As we will see later, the sacraments do give grace, but not the grace that leads to salvation. And in any event, the sacraments are themselves made effective by faith, so even in this case faith is the channel through which grace comes to us.) I should add that this is not the only way of formulating the Protestant position. In reality, grace comes through faith and faith comes from grace; they feed into each other, but together they lead to salvation.

Questioning Authority

Of the two principal issues that divided Catholics and Protestants, it might seem that their disagreements over how we are saved would be the most important. But in many ways, this was secondary to the more basic question of authority, that is, how do we find religious truth. All of theology hinges on how this question is answered. In the sixteenth century, there were essentially three approaches to this issue: the traditional Catholic approach, the approach of the humanists (who were generally reform-minded Catholics), and the approach of Luther and the Protestants. We will look at these in order.

Catholicism has held for centuries that there are two basic sources of authority in the church: Scripture and tradition. Scripture is the Bible, the Old and New Testaments plus the Apocrypha, a section of the Septuagint—the

Greek translation of the Old Testament—that neither Jews nor Protestants recognize as part of the Bible. In medieval times, the Bible was only available in a Latin translation made by St. Jerome in the fifth century (the Vulgate). Of course, the Bible needs to be interpreted in order for it to be useful for answering religious questions. In the Middle Ages, theologians had identified four senses of Scripture that were found in every passage: the literal sense (the least interesting), the spiritual (*anagogical*) sense, the moral (*allegorical*) sense, and a meaning related to human society (the *tropological* sense). For example, when found in the Bible, "Jerusalem" refers to: (1) a city in the Middle East (literal sense); (2) heaven, since Jerusalem was the city of God (anagogical sense); (3) an upright life, for the same reason (allegorical sense); and (4) political rule, since Jerusalem was the capital of Israel (tropological sense). In cases where the interpretation was not clear, Catholics could appeal to their second source of authority, tradition, to help clear up the problem.

Tradition is actually a much broader, more complex category than it sounds. It is based in part on the observation that most of what Jesus said and did was not in fact recorded in the Gospels, as John himself tells us (John 21:25). Yet, if you were one of the apostles, would you forget or ignore the many things Jesus taught you? Would you forget his words, his sermons, his private teachings? The words of the Son of God incarnate are so precious that you would not simply let them be forgotten, would you? Wouldn't you teach them to your followers, particularly those whom you designated leaders in the churches you founded? This was precisely the argument put forward by the early Christian writer Irenaeus to counter the claims of various gnostic heresies that claimed to have Jesus's secret oral teachings. These teachings would have been entrusted

41

to the leaders of the communities founded by the apostles, and through the apostolic succession of bishops, the orthodox church must be the custodian of these oral teachings. Over time, at least in the Latin West, apostolic succession became associated particularly with the church of Rome because, according to tradition, its first bishop was Peter, the head of the apostles.

But the concept of tradition goes well beyond simply the assumption of oral teaching entrusted to the early bishops. It is also based on Christ's promise that he would send the Holy Spirit to guide us into all truth (John 16:13). Tradition thus embodies the ongoing guidance of the Spirit in the church. This includes the writings of prominent Christian leaders and "saints," decisions and decrees of church councils, and particularly papal pronouncements, since the pope is the head of the church and the principle source of authority within it. Not all papal pronouncements are equally binding; as the theology would develop in the wake of the Reformation, the pope has to speak *ex cathedra,* from the throne of St. Peter, and has to express the consensus of the church in order for his pronouncement to be infallible. It is a power popes have rarely used.

Although tradition was a concept most Catholics were comfortable with, it raised problems for some of the reformers within the church, notably the humanists. First of all, many practices the humanists believed were superstitious, and many abuses within the church were justified using local or church tradition. Further, as indicated in the first chapter, the humanists were obsessed with the ancient world and wanted as much as possible to return to it as the source of knowledge and truth. Christian humanists applied this to the church and decided that it needed to be reformed following the model of early Christianity. In other words, the humanists argued that Scripture and the early Christian writers known as the church fathers were the only legitimate sources of authority in the church. After all, the church fathers were closer to Christ and in some cases had direct contact with the apostles. Surely they knew more about what Christ taught than later writers; surely their word should have more weight than the accretions that had been added to church teachings over the more recent centuries. The humanists thus maintained a notion of tradition, but for them it was a stripped-down version that was limited to the writers of the first few centuries of the Christian era.

As literary scholars, the humanists also objected to the approach to studying the Bible that had prevailed in the medieval world. As Greek and Hebrew texts of the Bible became increasingly available, Christian scholars picked up the language skills to study them. As we have seen in chapter 1, this led to calls by people such as Lorenzo Valla and Erasmus to reform or retranslate the Vulgate, a very controversial proposal since much medieval theology had been

built around long chains of reasoning based on the precise wording of the Vulgate. Some audacious individuals even began to translate portions of the Bible into the languages spoken by the common people, a task that would provoke even stronger reactions than the challenge to the Vulgate. The humanists also challenged the medieval approach to interpreting Scripture. Rather than arguing that all texts had four meanings, the humanists held that they had but a single meaning, which could be either literal or figurative depending on the context. This approach to the Bible again called into question the entire approach to scholarship of the scholastic theologians, who treated the Bible as a mine for propositions to be used in developing logical theological systems.

When Luther came along, he took the humanists' arguments to their logical conclusion. If you really want to get back to the origins of Christianity, the oldest and most authentic witness to the teachings of Jesus and the apostles, you have to go back to the Bible. Thus for Luther, Scripture alone (*sola scriptura*) is a legitimate source of authority in the church. Not only does the Bible contain the undiluted teachings of the apostles, but it was inspired by the Holy Spirit; it is thus infinitely more reliable than works by any other writers, no matter how close in date to the apostles. At the same time, however, although Luther rejected tradition as an independent source of authority in the church, he snuck it in the back door. He argued that at least some elements of church tradition were legitimate since they accurately reflect and summarize the teachings of Scripture. They are not directly authoritative, but nonetheless have a secondary degree of authority since they are based on the truly authoritative teachings of the Bible. Thus, for example, Luther used the creeds even though they are not found verbatim in Scripture.

The key problem, however, was interpreting the Bible. Like the humanists, Luther argued that Scripture had just one meaning, generally the literal meaning in the New Testament and a figurative meaning in the Old. To find the meaning, you use the more clear passages of Scripture to interpret the less clear. And for Luther, the clearest teaching in Scripture was salvation through Christ, by grace through faith; this was therefore the lens Luther used to interpret the entire Bible. Luther also believed in the perspicacity of Scripture, a fancy term that means that it is clear enough for people to understand the essence of its message. This meant that everyone had the right to study the Bible (and therefore to see that Luther was obviously correct). While in the Wartburg castle, along with directing the reform at Wittenberg from a distance and writing various tracts, treatises, and the like, Luther also translated the Bible into German. Unfortunately, Luther rapidly discovered that not everyone agreed with his interpretation of Scripture, and so he was forced to backpedal and to argue that only people trained in biblical studies (i.e., pastors and theologians) could interpret Scripture reliably. But it was too late, the genie was out of the bottle: Protestantism would rapidly fragment into a wide range of competing groups. We will look at that problem more in later chapters.

The Mysteries of the Faith

Although today we tend to think about the rise of Protestantism mostly in terms of the new religious ideas promulgated by Luther and other Protestant leaders, that is only one aspect of the Reformation, albeit a central one. Virtually all major Protestant leaders recognized that religion went beyond simply church teachings to liturgical practices.

Today, American evangelicals tend to think that the things we do in a worship service are mostly a matter of taste, that God doesn't particularly care what we do as long as we feel blessed by it. (This is much less true in many other branches of Protestantism with their roots more firmly in the period of the Reformation, such as the Anglicans/Episcopalians, Lutherans, and some Reformed churches.) In the sixteenth century, these ideas would be seen as sacrilege or blasphemy; worship is to be directed at God, not at making us feel good. It is in fact good for us, of course, but only because it involves a proclamation of God's truth and redirects our attention away from ourselves and toward the God who made us and saved us. Further, many evangelicals today don't give much thought to the sacraments: "Oh, is it Communion Sunday? I'd forgotten. The service will probably end up running a bit late." (Again, this tends not to be as true of the more traditional Protestant churches.) In fact, some churches don't even talk about sacraments at all, describing them instead as "ordinances," things God has "ordained" that we do but that in practice have little real impact on our faith or on our lives. This de-emphasis on the sacraments is largely a result of Enlightenment rationalism, with its radical split between the spiritual and the physical. This type of thinking makes it hard for people to believe that physical objects can really have spiritual significance or power, or that God particularly cares much about them or indeed about other elements in our worship.

In the sixteenth century, virtually everyone believed that the sacraments were essential to true Christianity and that sacramental practice flowed from right doctrine. To understand the how and why of this, we need to back up a bit and explain exactly what sacraments are, using ideas that were widely accepted within the period. The best place to start is with the Latin word *sacramentum,* which is a translation of the Greek work *mysterion,* meaning "a mystery," that is, something that has been hidden but is now revealed. This admittedly doesn't help us much, so perhaps we should turn to a simpler definition: A sacrament is "a visible sign of an invisible grace." To take this a bit further, we can use the words of Augustine, who described a sacrament as a visible promise. The idea is that God is way beyond our capacity to understand: He is infinite, we are finite; he is holy, we are sinful; he is spiritual, we are physical. Because of all this, we tend to be very slow to believe God's promises and to understand what he is saying to us. God, however, recognizes this and has graciously decided to meet us halfway; since we are physical and inevitably think in physical terms, God gives us physical signs to strengthen our faith in his promises. The "mystery" of the promise is thus made visible and clear to us. For example, God promises to forgive our sins through Christ, yet in

times of temptation or because we sin so often, we can find ourselves doubting that forgiveness and feeling overwhelmed by guilt. So to help us through these times, God gives us the sacrament of baptism, reminding us that just as the water "washed" our body, so our guilt has been washed away by Christ. (This is only one function of baptism, and only one promise that is connected to this sacrament. For example, Paul tells us that we have died and risen with Christ—a more difficult concept than God washing our sins away—and that baptism is a physical picture of this fact.)

In the case of the Lord's Supper, we have Jesus's words, "Unless you eat the flesh of the Son of Man and drink his blood, you have no life in you. Those who eat my flesh and drink my blood have eternal life, and I will raise them up on the last day" (John 6:53–54). Now think about that for a minute. Sometimes our familiarity with the Gospels makes us miss how weird some of the things that Jesus said actually were. This sounds an awful lot like we are dealing with ritual cannibalism, a charge brought against the early Christians by their Roman persecutors. No wonder Jesus lost lots of disciples when he said this! Obviously the text isn't meant to be taken literally; even the disciples that left must have known that. But what does it mean? One way of looking at it is to consider what eating and drinking does for us: It keeps us alive; it gives us our health, our strength, our energy. Without eating and drinking, we simply cannot do anything, even live. When we talk about "eating and drinking" Christ, we are to think of him in terms of food. Just as food sustains our bodies, so Christ is to be the source of our life. We are to draw our strength from him and to look to him as the one essential without whom we cannot survive, much less accomplish anything worthwhile. We eat and drink to keep us alive until the day we die; we draw life from Christ not only in this world but into eternity. Yet, however powerful this image is, it is difficult to grasp it and to live it out, tied as we are to the material world and being generally disinclined to see the spiritual side of life. So God graciously made this promise visible by giving us the Lord's Supper to provide a picture of drawing our nourishment from Christ. Just as the bread we eat and the wine we drink gives us life and health, so it is with Christ, who is the ultimate source of our life and health spiritually as well as physically.

So the point is that in the case of the two sacraments recognized by mainstream Protestants, they were given to us to be visible signs that help us understand and latch onto the promises that God has given us in Christ. A sacrament thus is a means of grace, since it strengthens our faith, which is the conduit through which God's grace comes to us. Obviously much more can be said about sacramental theology, including such issues as what promises are involved in the sacraments, what precisely they symbolize, the relationship between the sacramental sign and the thing it signifies, the number of sacraments, variations on the interpretation of the sacraments in general as well as of specific sacraments, and so forth. For now, though, we need to look at Luther's criticism of the Catholic Church's sacraments and his approach to sacramental reform. We will return to other aspects of the problem later.

Within Catholicism, there were a lot of ideas about what practices were or were not sacraments up until the 1200s. During this century, the church officially decided that there were seven, which acted as antidotes to the seven deadly sins (pride, greed, luxury, anger, gluttony, envy, and sloth, better translated as *depression* or *despair*). The seven sacraments within Catholicism are baptism, penance (or confession, or the sacrament of reconciliation), the

Eucharist (or Communion, or the Lord's Supper), confirmation, marriage, holy orders (roughly the equivalent of ordination), and extreme unction (anointing the sick, or last rites). Protestant reformers by and large rejected the notion that most of these were sacraments, arguing instead for a far more conservative use of the term. This was based largely on the Protestant principle of *sola scriptura*. Luther and most all other Protestant leaders argued that a sacrament was something that had been mandated by Christ himself, and about which we have enough information in Scripture to know how to do it correctly. This narrowed the list considerably.

Penance. Although Luther initially accepted penance as a sacrament, he soon rejected it. James 5:16 may tell us to confess our sins to one another, but the text does not spell out exactly what that means. For example, it does not specify that confession must be made to a priest, it does not tie forgiveness of sins to this confession (though Jas. 5:15 suggests that forgiveness may be tied into prayer), and it does not say that all sins must be specifically enumerated, which would be an impossible burden, according to Luther, given the pervasiveness of human sin. Further, the Catholic notion of penance rejects the complete adequacy of Christ's work on the cross for obtaining our salvation and thus the principles of *sola fide* and *sola gratia*. We do confess our sins individually, but we also do so collectively at the beginning of the worship service. And this is not a sacrament.

Confirmation and marriage. Confirmation is out as well; it is a good idea, according to Luther, and should be practiced, but it doesn't qualify as a sacrament since it is not mentioned anywhere in Scripture, whether by Christ or anyone else. Marriage is out too; pagans, Jews, and Muslims all marry, so how can it be a sacrament of the church? It is a creation ordinance, binding on all humanity since the time of Adam and Eve. No one would deny its importance, but it is not a sacrament.

Holy orders. There are plenty of examples of people in Scripture who were set aside for the work of the church with a special ceremony involving anointing with oil and the laying on of hands. And in fact, John Calvin said that it was proper to call ordination a sacrament. But in general most Protestants rejected the idea, partly because of the lack of both a clear command from Christ to ordain leaders and a clear indication of how to do it properly, but also because of a reaction to the Catholic notion of a priesthood that stood between the believer and God. Protestants argue that all believers are priests (1 Pet. 2:9) and have direct access to God, and thus there is no need for any mediator between God and humanity except Christ.

Extreme unction. Lastly, Luther and the Protestants also rejected extreme unction. Although James 5:14–15 tells us to call the elders of the church when we are sick for prayer and anointing with oil, Christ did not institute or command the practice and thus it cannot be a sacrament. Further, the passage in James does not mention people being on their deathbed; it implies that it is to be used on all the sick, so the concept of "last rites" cannot be drawn from this passage. Finally, if James's anointing of the sick were a sacrament, the promise attached to it would be healing, a promise that is rarely carried out in practice among those who receive it. So either God is failing to carry out what he promised in the sacrament—calling into question the whole notion of sacraments—or it isn't a sacrament at all. Some Protestants, notably the Huguenots, carried this rejection of extreme unction so far that they even rejected funeral services, which they argued promoted superstitions such as prayers for the dead.

Baptism and the Eucharist. So what does that leave us? Baptism and the Eucharist, both which were expressly commanded by Christ himself. These are the only two sacraments recognized by most Protestant churches. But this doesn't mean that we're out of the woods yet as far as the sacraments go; both of them would raise problems for the early Protestant churches, since not all Protestants understood these sacraments in the same way. In fact, ironically enough, the sacraments Christ instituted to promote unity within the church were in fact one of the major sources of division within Protestantism. We will look at the beginnings of the fragmentation of Protestantism and other related topics in the next chapter.

Questions for Discussion

1. Early on, Catholics argued that Luther's ideas on justification removed any incentive to live a holy life. If you were saved by faith regardless of works, why bother living a moral life? Luther responded that we should do so out of love of God, not out of hope for salvation. What do you think is the relationship between faith and works?

2. Where do we find authority today? Is the church's agenda set by Scripture, tradition, or contemporary sensibilities? What in your view should set the agenda?

3. Is there a difference between baptism and Communion on the one hand, and other things we do in the church on the other? Should there be? Why or why not?

CHAPTER FOUR

Divisions

Lutheranism proved to be an incredibly divisive force in the empire. A number of principalities accepted the new doctrines, though most of the empire did not. And Charles V, the Holy Roman Emperor, most pointedly rejected them. In fact, under his leadership, the empire attempted to outlaw Lutheranism altogether. This led a number of the Lutheran princes to issue a protest against the imperial decrees that condemned their religious beliefs, and thus they became known as "Protestants," that is, protesters. But wherever Protestant ideas spread, division followed, and not only between Catholics and Protestants. Some of these divisions involved political issues, some social justice, but most centered on the inevitable theological differences that arose with the elimination of external controls on the interpretation of Scripture. We will survey a number of

Melanchthon and Karlstadt were quite impressed with them, though Melanchthon was more than a little concerned about the fact that they rejected infant baptism. Karlstadt, however, accepted the Zwickau Prophets with open arms and rapidly radicalized his message under the inspiration of the newcomers. In particular, he introduced a number of radical and controversial innovations to the celebration of the Lord's Supper. Another leader of the Wittenberg church named Zwilling went even further. He incited mobs to smash statues and stained glass windows in churches, claiming that they were idolatrous, and led attacks on monks in the area. The violence spread rapidly, and Luther was forced to return to Wittenberg in March 1522 to restore order in the city. He was the only religious leader with enough stature to get things under control. Meanwhile, Elector Frederick issued a number of edicts banning iconoclasm (i.e., smashing religious images) and restoring more traditional liturgies in the churches. Luther and Frederick quieted things down fairly quickly, but the violent outbursts did much to hurt the reputation of Luther and his followers and actually slowed the pace of reform in the Saxon churches.

This was not the end of the movement begun by the Zwickau Prophets. A man named Thomas Muntzer who had been associated with them would rapidly take center stage in a massive social revolution that disrupted the entire Holy Roman Empire. Muntzer was a Catholic priest who had attended the Leipzig Debate and had been converted to Luther's views. As time went on, however, he split with Luther. Muntzer became convinced that Christ's second coming was at hand, and that he was a new Elijah, a prophet sent to free the peasants who were trapped in poverty and spiritual ignorance. Meanwhile, the peasants themselves were suffering as a result of large-scale economic changes that were occurring throughout Europe. Population was up, leading to greater demand for food; this led to rapid inflation of food prices but stagnation of prices for manufactured goods along with stagnant wages for artisans. As if this weren't enough, the influx of silver from the New World and the boom in silver mining in central Europe also contributed to inflationary pressures, though to a lesser extent than the population growth. To make a long story short, large landowners were hurt by these trends because, although they had the land to grow food, they were unwilling to pay the peasants enough to get them to work in the fields. So the landowners attempted to reestablish old systems of compulsory labor, dues, and rents that had not been used for two hundred years. The peasants, understandably, were pretty annoyed at this, and the conditions were ripe for a widespread uprising.

Into this situation walked Muntzer, the self-proclaimed prophet sent to deliver the peasants from their oppressors. Under his influence, revolts began to spread like wildfire across the empire, with over 300,000 participants at their height. The peasants demanded relief from their economic plight—an end to serfdom, increased hunting and fishing rights, impartial law courts—as well as religious reforms, such as the right to select their own pastors, the right collect their own tithes (the 10 percent of their produce they owed to the church), and the right to select their own bishops. (Actually, it is not clear the peasants really wanted these religious reforms; they may have been added by the clerics who acted as the peasants' spokesmen.) Luther initially urged moderation; the lords had mistreated the peasants, though the peasants should not have acted so insolently. He changed his tune after a trip to Thuringia, which he undertook at great personal risk to try to bring the revolt to an end without violence. He was so frightened by what he saw there, however, that when he returned he wrote a pamphlet urging the lords to put the revolt down speedily and to use all necessary force to do so. A combined Catholic/Lutheran army led by Philip of Hesse met the peasants at Frankenhausen in 1525. There, using all the weapons in their arsenal (including artillery) the lords slaughtered almost the entire peasant army. Muntzer, who promised that the peasants would be unharmed and that he would catch the nobility's cannonballs in the sleeves of his coat, was found hiding disguised in a nearby hut; he was given a speedy trial and beheaded. I should perhaps note that after the slaughter Luther bitterly regretted his impulsive words on the peasant revolt and condemned the brutality with which it was ended. Unfortunately, however, his words gave at least the Lutherans the excuse they needed to massacre the participants. Luther has been condemned for this tract ever since; his too-late repentance does little to excuse his words.

However much Luther may have condemned the nobility's actions at Frankenhausen, neither he nor any other leading thinkers of the day, Catholic or Protestant alike, had anything good to say about people like the Zwickau Prophets or Thomas Muntzer who claimed direct divine revelation; for example, in a 1525 tract, Luther commented that these so-called prophets had "swallowed the Holy Spirit, feathers and all." Luther's insistence on *sola scriptura* was intended to counter not only Catholic reliance on tradition but the "spiritualists" (the term historians and sociologists use to describe groups or individuals who claim direct divine inspiration) as well. Unfortunately, however, reliance on Scripture as the ultimate source of authority raised other problems with both reform-minded Catholics and other Protestants alike.

Luther and Erasmus

As we saw in chapter 1, Luther wasn't the only game in town when it came to church reform. In fact, even before Luther got rolling, another reform movement was under way, led by Dutch humanist Desiderius Erasmus, that came very close to cleaning up the Catholic Church from within. Erasmus's reform, which had gained quite a bit of support within the church hierarchy, was based on a return to the sources of the Christian faith—the Bible and the church fathers (i.e., early Christian writers)—and was especially concerned with ending corruption and correcting abuses in church practices. When Luther came along, he attacked many of the same abuses as Erasmus, although Luther argued that these were secondary issues. For him, the basic problem in the church was doctrine: The Catholics had lost the gospel of salvation by grace through faith alone, and all of the other problems in the church stemmed from that betrayal of the truth. As Luther's fame grew, it was inevitable that his relationship with Erasmus, the most prominent reformer in the church, would become an issue with which they would both have to deal.

Though he sympathized with much that Luther said, particularly his criticism of abuses in the church, Erasmus found Luther's bull-in-a-china-shop approach too abrasive for his tastes. The Dutch humanist tried to sit on the fence while both sides courted his support, arguing in essence that Luther's attacks on abuses of practice were appropriate, though his breaking of the unity of the church was wrong and his emphasis on doctrinal issues was misplaced. Erasmus had little patience with theological arguments; these amounted in his mind to logical hairsplitting, something no self-respecting humanist tolerated. Ultimately, however, the Catholic authorities forced him to take a stand, and so Erasmus rather reluctantly wrote *On the Freedom of the Will,* an attack on a number of aspects of Luther's theology. This book argued, in good humanist fashion, that Luther was far too pessimistic about human ability, that original sin did not permeate us as thoroughly as Luther had said, and that our actions do have a role to play in our salvation. The implication in this, of course, was that Luther's reform program was flawed at its very roots, and that Erasmus's practice-oriented approach was far superior, since human actions do in fact count before God. Luther replied with *On the Bondage of the Will,* arguing that Erasmus was reviving the ancient Christian heresy of Pelagianism in his defense of human freedom. Luther went so far as to say that Erasmus's book only succeeded in convincing him that he was right. All of Erasmus's eloquence could not disguise the fact that his ideas were unoriginal and worthless; using such remarkable eloquence to make such arguments was like "using gold or silver dishes to carry garden rubbish or dung." Needless to say, the split between the Catholic humanist reformers and Luther was permanent.

Meanwhile, Erasmus found that he had sat on the fence too long. Neither side trusted him, and the Catholic reaction against Luther made even Erasmus's humanistic reform program suspect in the eyes of the church. Luther had changed all the rules as far as the church was concerned. Now anyone criticizing even clearly abusive practices in the church was suspected of being a closet Lutheran. In Erasmus's case, his criticism of the church and his humanist methodology in studying the Bible led people to criticize him for "laying the egg that Luther hatched." His antipathy toward formal theology didn't help either. He was neither fish nor fowl; he criticized abuses in the church much like Luther did yet claimed to be a good Catholic, while at the same time hardly discussing the issues that Luther raised and dodging the real questions at the heart of the controversy as much as possible. He was about as hard to nail down as jello. This contributed to his somewhat undeserved reputation for prevarication. The general attitude toward him has been that where Luther said, "Here I stand," Erasmus said, "Here I stand. And here. And here. And here . . ."

Although they advocated fundamentally different approaches to reform, however, there was some important common ground between the two. Erasmus came very close to Luther's position on authority; the Bible was fundamental, though Erasmus gave greater weight to early Christian writers than Luther did. The common emphasis on returning to the sources of the faith should not be

Although Zwingli's and Luther's doctrines were quite similar, the Swiss reformer emphasized preaching and teaching the Bible even more than did Luther. Among other things, this meant that Zurich had a much more austere approach to worship. Images and organs were removed from churches as being either idolatrous or a distraction from the pure preaching of the Word, the liturgy was greatly simplified, and only psalms were sung during worship (and *a capella* at that) despite the fact that Zwingli was an accomplished lutenist and probably the most talented musician of any of the Reformers. Zwingli's humanist training also made him more concerned with external behavior than Luther, whose background in the monastery made him allergic to giving "works" any role in religion except as an expression of thanks to God. Zwingli pushed

for the creation of a joint church-state court to handle questions related to marriage (previously reserved for Catholic ecclesiastical courts) and morals. Both of these elements—liturgical austerity and a system of enforcement of morality—would continue to be important elements in the Reformed tradition (essentially, the branches of Protestantism that have their roots in Switzerland) as it developed over the next several decades.

The Anabaptists

Though Zwingli's reform program may have been more radical in some respects than Luther's, there were critics in Zurich who thought that it didn't go far enough. The most significant of these was a group known as the Swiss Brethren, led by Conrad Grebel. The Swiss Brethren rejected the notion of reforming the church altogether, arguing that the church was so hopelessly corrupt that reform was impossible. Instead, the church needed to return to the model of the book of Acts, where the church existed as a voluntaristic community of faith in an evil world. The mainstream reformers argued that since religion was the foundation of society, the church needed to be integrated into society's political and social structures as was done in ancient Israel; Grebel and his followers argued that this was Judaizing (i.e., returning to Judaism), and that Christians needed to follow the New Testament rather than the Old. Put simply, people needed to understand what they were doing when they joined the church. Church membership was not for everyone, but only for those who could make a credible profession of faith and who then live that faith out in their lives. If you failed to toe the line, you would be expelled from the community ("banned" or "shunned") so that no one (including your pastor named Bernhard Rothmann. Meanwhile, a radical Protestant named Melchior Hoffmann whose main emphasis was millennarianism—that Christ's return was at hand—had collected a group of followers; he was thrown in prison, however, and died there. His followers took his death as a martyrdom, the persecution that confirmed that Christ was going to come back any minute, and so they looked for a place they could go and wait for him. Since in Münster Rothmann was growing more radical in his thinking, they decided to head there. The influx of radicals caused the locals to flee, which led to the city being taken over by a group of extremists led by Jan van Leiden and Jan Matthijs. They forced Rothmann out and imposed a dictatorship of the saints on the city. They set up a new government with new rituals, established a draconian law code (e.g., you could be executed for swearing), enforced rebaptism, and—following the example of the biblical patriarchs—made polygamy mandatory. At this point a combined Roman Catholic/Lutheran army moved in to deal with a situation neither side could tolerate. The city was besieged and very nearly starved into submission until a few of its residents slipped out and showed the besiegers how to get in to the city. A bloody sack followed; the leaders were captured, tortured to death, and their bodies were put in a cage and hung from the steeple of the church, where they remained until the twentieth century.

Münster rapidly became a byword among the mainstream churches, used to tar anyone whose ideas were more radical than one's own. Catholics said that as soon as one accepted Lutheran ideas, it led inevitably toward the kind of chaos that took place in Münster; Lutherans said no, they helped deal with Münster, and that the problem was the Zwinglians who spawned the Anabaptists; the Zwinglians argued that they had thrown the Anabaptists out, and that it was the fault of the Swiss Brethren. As for the Anabaptists themselves, the reaction of one Menno Simons to Münster is perhaps the most important. Menno was a Dutch priest who converted to the Anabaptist cause. He was sickened by what he saw in Münster; he even lost some friends there. So he turned away from violence altogether and advocated radical pacifism, though he did retain the extreme disciplinary practices of the Anabaptists, including the ban. (Later, the Amish would break off from the Mennonites on the grounds that they were not strict enough.)

There were loads of other Anabaptists and other types of radical groups in the sixteenth century, but for present purposes we'll leave it here. We do need to note one other major division among Protestants, however, that would have a far more systematic and widespread impact than the largely isolated and localized groups of radicals: the split between Luther and Zwingli over the Lord's Supper. We will look at that in the next chapter.

Questions for Discussion

1. Some of the earliest divisions within Protestantism came about because of political issues, whether on the part of the knights or the peasants. Is it possible to separate religion and politics? Should the church take a stand on social issues that the state must inevitably address? If so, how should we define the relationship between church and state?

2. With the absence of a central authority guiding biblical interpretation, a number of competing Protestant traditions have developed. Is it possible for them to work together while maintaining their distinct theologies, or must they agree that their differences don't matter in order to participate in ecumenical activities? What are

A Fork in the Road

Zwingli's reform program proved to be very popular in the German-speaking parts of Switzerland and in many of the Imperial Free Cities, particularly in the southern parts of the empire. Lutheranism tended to spread into states within the empire governed by princes. Eventually, the two flavors of Protestantism collided. Several issues divided them, but two stood out: the style of worship (Zwinglians were more austere, whitewashing churches and removing art work, organs, etc., whereas Lutherans were freer about using these as part of worship), and the interpretation of the Lord's Supper. Eventually, the disagreements between the two sides became so heated that Elector Frederick of Saxony, Luther's patron and protector, feared that if Zwingli and Luther continued to quarrel it would enable the emperor's Catholic forces to wipe out Protestantism altogether, piece by piece. (As Benjamin Franklin was later to note about the American Revolution, "If we do not hang together, we will most assuredly hang separately.") So to try to reestablish a united Protestant front against the Catholic emperor, the Elector arranged for Luther and Zwingli to meet in the city of Marburg in 1529 to discuss their differences.

The Marburg Colloquy was hardly a rousing success. The two sides reached agreement fairly quickly on nearly all issues that separated them. They agreed, for example, that religious images should not be destroyed, in part because such action promoted violence and mob rule; they agreed that each side had the freedom under Christ to conduct worship services as it saw fit; they agreed on the basic tenets of the gospel, on *sola scriptura,* and on all of the other key doctrinal points that distinguished Protestants from Catholics. But they drew the line at the Lord's Sup-

per. Luther reportedly took out his knife (carried by everyone in those days for eating, miscellaneous cutting chores, self-defense, etc.) and carved on the table, *Hoc est corpus meum* ("This is my body" in Latin); he said that Christ said that the bread was his body and that was good enough for Luther. Zwingli replied that "is" did not always mean "equals"; sometime it means "represents" in Scripture. Luther replied that that was true, but it wasn't the case here. Zwingli pointed out that Christ's body is seated at the right hand of God the Father Almighty, as it says in the creed; it thus can't be "in, with, and under" the bread all over the world since a body cannot be in many places at once. To argue that Christ's body can be in many places at once denies his true humanity by "violating the nature of bodies" and by confusing his human nature with his divine nature. Luther replied that Christ's body can be everywhere since God is omnipotent, and to deny this denies Christ's divinity. And so on. At the end of the discussion, they issued a very positive statement listing their agreement on all points under dispute except this one, on which they

would hold further discussions in anticipation of reaching agreement soon. This was, in point of fact, a bald-faced lie. Neither side expected to reach agreement, and before the ink was dry on the document they each returned home and started issuing tracts attacking the other.

Ultimately, the Marburg Colloquy was a turning point in the Reformation, marking the definitive split between the Lutheran and the Reformed (or "Sacramentarian") branches of Protestantism. The two sides have never been able to come to agreement since, and other issues have arisen to further divide the two groups. The long-term consequences of this division are difficult to exaggerate. The Lutheran insistence on a view of the Lord's Supper that virtually no other reformers of the period agreed with meant that Lutherans became increasingly isolated from the growth of Protestantism outside of the empire and Scandinavia, particularly since they had a tendency to attack anyone who disagreed with a very narrow interpretation of their views. These differences would be major contributing factors to the Thirty Years' War, a conflict that drew nearly all the countries west of the Turkish Empire and the Russias into the most bloody and destructive war in history to that point.

On the other hand, given the Protestant principle of *sola scriptura,* in retrospect such divisions seem almost inevitable. The lack of an authoritative interpretation of Scripture meant that there was no effective mechanism for settling differences of opinion over the meaning of the biblical text. And since Protestants saw the Reformation as centering on Word and Sacrament, that is, the message of the gospel and the correct interpretation of the sacraments, these issues were the inevitable battlegrounds not only between Catholic and Protestant but between Protestant and Protestant as well. Even if you got the gospel right, if

you got the sacraments wrong, you were not part of a true church, and thus division was necessary.

The Spread of Reformed Protestantism

Although best remembered as a religious reformer, Zwingli was also involved in moral and political causes as well. Ultimately, a combination of all three would lead both to limits on the spread of his religious reform and to his death.

From early in his career, Zwingli had been concerned with the Swiss practice of providing mercenary infantry to a variety of political leaders, most notably the king of France and the pope. The Swiss Guards at the Vatican today are descendants of these mercenaries. The Swiss infantry had a reputation for being unbeatable (despite experience to the contrary), and thus they were in high demand among those who could pay for them. For their part, the Swiss by and large viewed this as a good business opportunity; many of the cantons made quite a bit of money exporting their young men as soldiers, most of whom would return richer than they had left. Zwingli, however, considered this trade to be terribly immoral. Why should the Swiss die for the king of France? Just so the canton could make money? What kind of people sells the blood of its youth for gold? Zwingli devoted a great deal of energy to trying to end this practice. The canton of Zurich withdrew from the mercenary trade, causing real resentment on the part of the other Swiss cantons, who feared that if Zwingli's ideas spread, it could result in the end of a lucrative trade.

And spread Zwingli's ideas did. Even prior to the Marburg Colloquy, many of the Imperial Free Cities, especially in the Rhineland, and some of the Swiss cantons converted

to Zwinglianism. Many of Zwingli's supporters came from the ranks of his fellow humanists who converted to Protestantism, in some cases more under the influence of Luther than of Zwingli himself. For example, Franz von Sickingen, the leader of the Knights' Revolt, and his spokesman, the humanist Ulrich von Hutton, led a circle of reform-minded humanists that included Martin Bucer, a Dominican theologian, and Johannes Oecolampadius. These two were heavily influenced by Erasmus, as was Wolfgang Capito, another humanistically inclined reformer. Capito and Bucer, together with Matthew Zell, began a Zwinglian-influenced reform movement in Strasbourg. Bucer had developed his own approach to theology, and though influenced by Zwingli, continued to maintain an independent, distinctive approach to theology that sought to bridge the gap between Zwingli and Luther. The city council of Strasbourg decided to convert the city to Protestantism by 1521. Under Bucer's influence the city ultimately adopted a more-or-less Reformed approach to theology that nonetheless allowed for a great deal of diversity in religious practice; Lutherans, Zwinglians, and even some Anabaptists were all tolerated in the city. Capito and Bucer were then involved in preparing church orders for various south German cities together with a confession of faith, the Tetrapolitan Confession (i.e., "Four Cities Confession": Strasbourg, Constance, Lindau, Memmingen). Although theologically Reformed, Bucer and Capito never really left their Erasmian roots. Rather than taking a confrontational or combative stance on their positions, they worked very hard to try to bring the Reformed and Lutheran sides together, as evidenced by the relative toleration of Strasbourg. Bucer even attempted to find common ground with the Catholics, something most other Reformers refused to do, since they believed that the pope was the antichrist.

Bucer also was very involved in international Protestantism, being one of the first reformers to take an active interest in promoting the budding Protestant movement in France and helping to found a French refugee church in Strasbourg. We will return to Bucer and this church later when we discuss John Calvin.

Oecolampadius was influenced by Luther early on, but by the time he was appointed to be pastor of St. Martin's Church in Basel, he had shifted toward Zwingli's theology. Capito and several others—including Erasmus, ironically—had been preparing the Basel reform for some time. Reports of the Peasant War and the threat of the Anabaptists slowed the acceptance of Protestant ideas in the city, however. Meanwhile in Bern, the largest and militarily the most powerful canton in Switzerland, had been moving toward Protestantism through the work of Berchthold Haller, a humanist friend of Melanchthon and teacher in Bern. In 1528, Zwingli, Oecolampadius, Bucer, and Capito conducted a disputation in the city, and the city council decided to convert the canton to Reformed Protestantism. This was a major coup for Zwingli; even the king of France, the wealthiest and most populous kingdom in Europe, was hesitant to do anything to annoy Bern, given the strength of its military. Bernese support for Reformed Protestantism thus helped protect the movement from powers that might have wished to destroy it. And with Bern converted, Basel followed suit the next year, with Oecolampadius as the *antistes,* or head, of the Basler church.

The interconnections between Oecolampadius, Capito, and Bucer go even deeper than these common reform projects, however; they all married in succession a woman by the name of Wilibrandis Rosenblatt. Wilibrandis was the widow of a man named Ludwig Keller. She married Oecolampadius in 1528; after he died, she married Capito, and

when he died, Bucer. When Bucer died in 1551, she remained unmarried until her death in 1564.

These are only a few examples of the spread of Reformed Protestantism. The important question at this point is why some territories converted to Lutheranism and others to Reformed ideas. Personal connections between reformers such as those outlined above undoubtedly helped, but there was more involved than simply networking. Theology was another element; Luther and his followers refused to accept anyone who would not agree with their specific interpretation of the Lord's Supper, an interpretation that was unacceptable to the majority of reformers. The differences in the environments in which Zwingli's and Luther's ideas spread is another part of the puzzle. As we have seen, Zwinglianism was an urban religion; it appealed to the south German cities in the Rhineland and to the capitals of the Swiss mountain cantons. Lutheranism, in contrast, spread primarily within the larger territorial units within the empire under the authority of Protestant princes. There are several reasons why this difference may be important. The higher literacy rates in the cities may have made the more austere, word-centered style of worship of Zwinglianism more attractive than the liturgical drama of Catholicism and, to some extent, Lutheranism. Further, the cities may have wanted to reinforce the moral center of the community, thus making Zwingli's church-state courts and emphasis on discipline attractive. Still another element may be the differences in structure between the two churches. Lutheran churches tended to adopt a form of church government based on bishops, albeit with drastically reduced powers; this type of hierarchical structure mirrored the structure of the state government in the territorial states ruled by princes. Towns, on the other hand, were typically governed by var-

ious types of councils, a structure that was also present in most Zwinglian and Reformed church orders. The political powers that decided whether to become Protestant and, if so, which form of Protestantism to adopt would have found much more in common with the church whose structure reinforced their own authority in the community. Whatever the reason, Reformed Protestantism spread widely and provided an alternative vision of Protestantism that would eventually surpass Lutheranism in influence.

Along with Bern, several of the other mountain cantons converted to a Zwinglian style of Protestantism, though not all of them willingly. Zwingli was not above using political pressure to push Zurich's smaller, weaker neighbors into adopting Protestantism in the hope that by converting the cantons—whether by political pressure or persuasion—Zurich would emerge as the leader of the Swiss Confederacy. Needless to say, other cantons did not see this as a positive thing, including Bern, Zurich's erstwhile ally and a

strongly Protestant state itself. The situation was further complicated by Zurich's withdrawal from the mercenary trade and the resentments this fostered among the other cantons. The five forest cantons set up an alliance to oppose the spread of Protestantism and later allied themselves with Austria, the traditional enemy of the Swiss. Tensions continued to rise. Thinking an all-out Catholic attack was imminent, Zwingli urged the Protestant cantons to attack the Catholic cantons in February 1531. War broke out, but because the cause involved more than just religion (notably the political ambitions of Zurich, as well as the issue of the mercenary trade), Bern stood on the sidelines. The war was over quickly; on October 10 the combined armies of the forest cantons met the army of Zurich in battle at Kappel, and the Protestant forces were routed. Zwingli, acting as chaplain and standard bearer for Zurich, was killed on the battlefield, and when his body was found the next day, it was dismembered and burned with dung by the victorious Catholic forces. (Much has been made of the fact that Zwingli was in armor during the battle; as a man of God, it is said, he had no business bearing arms. However, Swiss custom was that military chaplains wore armor without carrying weapons, so this charge against Zwingli is not really fair.)

Kappel was a disaster for Zurich and for the advance of Protestantism in Switzerland. Zurich's ambition to become the dominant power in Switzerland was ended; territories pressured into Protestantism were permitted to return to Rome; Catholic cantons were not to be targets for missionary activity. The mercenary trade continued as well. But Swiss Protestantism was still alive and well. Bern remained strong, and Zurich continued to play a major role in international Protestantism under its new religious leader, Zwingli's son-in-law Heinrich Bullinger.

The Changing of the Guard

Bullinger faced a difficult situation on his rise to the leadership of the Zurich church. Zurich was bankrupt and in no position to exert the kind of influence on the other Swiss cantons that it had before Kappel. There was even fear that it would be re-Catholicized. Bullinger stepped into this situation and navigated the challenges with a cool head and without the belligerence of Zwingli. He wrote a decree issued by the city council that reaffirmed Zurich's adherence to Reformed Protestantism. He then worked out a deal with the council that gave the Zurich synod the right to oversee the clergy under the authority of the town council, and the council sole right to administer discipline within the community. Bullinger's real efforts were devoted to pastoral leadership, however, both in Zurich and beyond. In his first ten years after Kappel, he preached six to eight sermons a week (reduced to two in 1542), as well as being director of the Zurich Academy until 1537 and professor of theology through the rest of his career. He was also an astonishingly prolific writer, producing the *Decades* (a collection of a hundred sermons), a history of the Reformation in Zurich, commentaries, published sermons, and 12,000 surviving letters to correspondents all over Europe. Perhaps most importantly, Bullinger was a principal author of the First and Second Helvetic Confessions, the latter being among the most widely accepted Reformed Confessions of the sixteenth century. Even when Zurich lost its political clout and as a result some of its role as leader of the Reformed world, the widespread respect enjoyed by Bullinger and his influence as a theologian preserved a central role for Zurich for decades to come.

Nonetheless, the leadership of the Reformed world was beginning to shift. In 1536, five years after Kappel, a city on Lac Leman in Savoy broke away from the prince-bishop who controlled it and converted to Protestantism under the influence of Bern. That city, Geneva, would eventually join the Swiss Confederation and become the preeminent city in the Protestant world under the direction of a French refugee, John Calvin. Events in Germany and elsewhere would lead to important changes in the Protestant world before Calvin's period of greatest influence, however, so we must turn now to those events, starting with internal reform movements within the Catholic Church.

Questions for Discussion

1. How important do you think sacramental interpretation is to Christian unity? Are the sacraments fundamental to the church, or are they add-ons? How much can we differ on them and still consider ourselves one in Christ?
2. Can spiritual grace be conveyed via physical objects?
3. Of the reasons suggested for the spread of Reformed Protestantism, which do you find the most convincing? Why?

CHAPTER SIX

Catholic Reform or Counter-Reform?

The Catholic Church didn't simply roll over and play dead during the years Protestantism was growing, though it did take time before the church mounted an effective response to the need for reform from within and the challenge of Protestantism from without. Part of the reason for this delay was rivalries within Catholicism. Erasmus had promoted the most viable program of reform within the church, but the combination of jealousy from professional theologians plus the suspicion that Erasmus had aided and abetted Luther effectively discredited the humanist and set the reform program back decades. Charles V and others tried to pressure the popes to call a council of the entire church to deal with Luther, but the popes dragged their feet; they did not want to risk a council that could threaten their power, and they certainly refused to hold one in Germany as the emperor demanded because that would give Charles too much pull in the council. At the same time, Charles had his problems politically and militarily. He was fighting against the Ottoman Turks, who were expanding into southeastern Europe, and against France and the pope. Meanwhile, Luther was miles ahead of his opponents in effective use of the printing press, the first means of mass communication in history, with the result that Protestant ideas spread very quickly across much of Europe and more and more cities and territories split with Rome. The net result was that well into the 1530s, Protestantism was advancing and Catholicism was largely in disarray.

But it didn't stay that way. Beginning with the pontificate of Paul III (1534–1549), the Catholic Church increasingly got its act together, so that by the end of the century, Protestantism had pretty much stopped expanding and many territories that had converted to Protestantism were re-Catholicized. Because of the timing, nineteenth-century historians referred to this process as the "Counter Reformation," seeing it as a response to Protestantism. Many Catholic and some Protestant historians cried foul at this terminology, arguing instead that the reforms instituted during the period were a result of internal developments within Catholicism and had nothing to do with Protestantism. They preferred to label the movement the "Catholic Reformation." Other historians prefer not to use either term, since many elements of the Catholic Church were untouched by reform in either sense during the period. They prefer the term "early modern Catholicism," though I personally think that term is too general to be of much use. Given the choice, most historians today will go with "Catholic Reformation," while recognizing that some elements of the Catholic Reformation were prompted by Protestantism—in other words, if you want to use the term, the "Counter Reformation" is a subset of the broader Catholic Reformation. That is the terminology we will use here.

New Religious Orders

Historically, any time the Catholic Church needed reforming, religious orders led the way. In some cases, reforming movements arose within existing orders with an eye to returning to the ideals of the founder; in other cases, entirely new orders were founded. Both processes occurred during the Catholic Reformation. Revitalized orders were particularly common in Spain, where mystics such as Theresa of Ávila led reform programs in their orders. The most important changes, however, came from new orders and confraternities (groups of laity who followed a structured program of religious exercises and service, sort of like a lay religious order). One of the most important of these was the Italian Oratory of Divine Love, founded in Genoa in 1497 and built around the ideas of St. Catherine of Genoa (1457–1510). It was lay dominated, and featured spiritual exercises, group prayer, frequent reception of the sacraments, and service to the poor. The Oratory spread to Rome in 1510, where some of its clerical members founded another quasi-religious order known as the Theatines in 1524. The Theatines were a group of priests dedicated to reforming the secular clergy (i.e., priests who were not members of a religious order). They lived a very austere life, being prohibited from either owning property or begging, and were dedicated to strict observance of canon law and to charity. Although they did not have many houses, the Theatines included a number of very influential members, such as Thomas de Vio (later Cardinal Cajetan) and Gian Pietro Caraffa (later Pope Paul IV), and had an impact on the church out of all proportion to their numbers.

Although these confraternities were founded during this period, the church was generally reluctant to create new religious orders. The feeling was that there were quite enough already, thank you, and if they weren't doing their job, they needed to be shut down or cleaned up. Despite the opposition, however, a few new orders were founded during the 1520s and '30s. The Capuchins began in 1528 as a reformed Franciscan order dedicated to following the example of Christ and St. Francis and committed to preaching the gospel wherever it was needed; they were officially recognized by Paul III in 1536. The Ursulines, an order for women devoted to virginity and charity, were founded in Brescia in 1535. And then there was the Society of Jesus, a new religious order that deserves a section of its own.

Ignatius Loyola and the Society of Jesus

The Society of Jesus, a.k.a. the Jesuits, was founded by Ignatius Loyola (c. 1491–1556). Loyola, the son of a nobleman, was a soldier whose military career came to an abrupt end when his leg was badly broken at the siege of Pamplona in 1521. He had an extended convalescence at a monastery called Montserrat due to the fact that his leg had been set badly and needed to be rebroken. He was getting pretty bored lying around, but he couldn't find anything worth reading. He was interested in chivalric

romances, but he was in a monastery, and all he could find in it was "women's books"—meaning devotional readings. Out of desperation, however, he started reading and got hooked. After recovering, he spent a year at a monastery at Manresa (outside of Barcelona), where he experienced visions and developed his *Spiritual Exercises,* a program of prayer and meditation based on the books he had read at Montserrat. The exercises were designed to promote a wholehearted commitment to Christ and to the church. Loyola then completed a pilgrimage to Jerusalem and went back to school to study theology. He needed to learn Latin first, of course, so this veteran soldier start taking classes with children to master the language. He eventually made it to the Collège Montaigu at the University of Paris, where the charismatic Loyola attracted a group of six men around him. Loyola led them through his *Spiritual Exercises,* and they took vows of poverty and chastity. Some time later, they set off on a pilgrimage to Jerusalem. They only made it as far as Venice, however, since the Turks made further travel too dangerous. They were ordained as priests, and in 1540 traveled to Rome to petition the pope to admit them as a new religious order. Over some opposition, Paul III agreed, and the Society of Jesus was born.

The Jesuits were an unusual order in several respects. First, they were all ordained priests and were very highly educated. Second, in addition to the standard monastic vows of poverty, chastity, and obedience (or "no money, no honey, and no funny"), they took a special fourth vow of obedience to the pope, going without question or delay anywhere he would send them. This may have tipped the scales in their favor with Paul III. This enabled popes to circumvent the usual rules of the order at need and made the Jesuits something like a SWAT team that the pope could use to address particularly thorny problems. Third, since they had to be free to travel, they were exempted from the liturgical responsibilities of normal religious orders, and even from the jurisdiction of local bishops who otherwise oversaw the monasteries and religious houses in their diocese. This enabled the Jesuits to base their spirituality on the *Spiritual Exercises* done as a month-long retreat under a spiritual director rather than on the liturgy and canonical hours of the traditional regular clergy.

In the late sixteenth century, the Jesuits worked in three main areas. The first was education. Jesuits were involved in preparing catechisms and basic devotional material for children and lay people, and eventually began establishing their own colleges and universities to provide high quality education to the young men who attended them. Although the schools taught mostly Catholic students, they had a missionary intent as well: Protestant parents, knowing that their children could get a high-powered, up-to-date education on the cheap in Jesuit schools and universities, often sent their sons to study in them. Protestant pastors did their best to stop this practice, fearing (rightly) that the schools would also try to win their Protestant students to Catholicism. But the pastors had only limited success. Protestant students attended Jesuit schools in substantial numbers, and many were converted to Catholicism. Meanwhile, the Jesuits were famous for boasting that if they had a boy by the time he was twelve, they would have him for life.

A second area of activity for the Jesuits was missions. Although by the seventeenth century Jesuits were involved in missions to the Americas, their initial work was in advanced cultures such as China and Japan. When they entered these territories, they did their best to use the culture to present themselves in a favorable light, adopting the clothing of Confucian sages in China for example. They would then use Western technologies that were different from those in their host country to open doors for them to the people in power in the country. Mechanical clocks were a favorite for this, though occasionally the practice could result in unexpected consequences. For example, one Jesuit was summoned to the imperial palace in China after presenting a clock to the emperor. The clock had broken, and the Jesuit was told he had one day to fix it or he would lose his head. Even with such problems, the Jesuits found this a useful approach; it enabled them to create alliances with the ruling classes, with the expectation that conversion of this group would lead to conversion of the masses. Ironically, the biggest opposition the Jesuits faced was from the Franciscans, whose missionaries thought that the Jesuits went way too far in accommodating local practices, such as allowing Chinese Christians to continue to burn incense to their ancestors, rationalizing this as an application of the commandment to "honor your father and your mother." The Franciscans protested to Rome about it. Eventually, this and other similar issues would lead to a full-blown conflict known as the Chinese Rites Controversy. To make a long story short, the Franciscans won, and the Jesuits were prohibited from compromising too much with local culture and language.

The third major area of Jesuit activity was in politics. Although the Jesuit constitution prohibited them from being involved in political affairs, this could be circumvented in a number of ways, particularly if the pope gave his approval. The main way Jesuits influenced politics was essentially the same approach they used on the mission field: They set up alliances with noblemen and kings by acting as their confessors, and from that position they sought to influence the religious policies of the kingdom. This approach was particularly effective in France, enabling the Jesuits to push the king to support the ultra-Catholic side during some of the Wars of Religion. With papal approval, the Jesuits could go even further; they were actually involved in assassination plots against Elizabeth I in England, with the goal of putting her (Catholic) cousin Mary Queen of Scots on the throne (see chapter 11).

Humanist Reform

Despite Erasmus's fall into disfavor, humanists influenced by the Dutch reformer continued to play an important role in the Catholic hierarchy. Paul III appointed a number of reform-minded cardinals, including Contarini, Sadoleto (who would later be involved in correspondence with Geneva that led to Calvin's return to the city), and the Theatine Gian Pietro Caraffa, who would later be elected Pope Paul IV. These three, together with a number of others who represented different approaches to reform, were named to a commission looking into the state of the church. Their 1537 report, entitled *Consilium de emendanda ecclesia* ("Council for the reform of the church"), was a succinct summary of the widespread abuses in the church, and laid the responsibility for them squarely on the papacy. Unfortunately, Paul III took no action in response to the council's findings. Even more unfortunately, the supposedly confidential report was leaked. It was printed in Rome, and the following year appeared in German translation with a preface by Luther. This didn't do anything to improve its popularity with the curia.

But Paul III and his humanist cardinals did not throw in the towel at this point. The humanists, particularly Contarini, believed that they could reach an agreement with more moderate Protestants such as Luther's protégé Melanchthon on the basis of their shared humanist training and (presumed) values. This is another indication that the humanist reformers didn't get it; for most Protestants, the problem was doctrine, not shared values or reform of practice. Nonetheless, Catholic and Protestant leaders held a series of disputations and colloquies in Speyer, Hagenau, Worms, Regensburg, and Leipzig (1540–1541). The most important of these was the Regensburg Colloquy (1541), attended in its early sessions by the emperor as well as by Melanchthon, Calvin (as an observer), the stridently anti-Luther Eck, and the humanist Contarini. Both sides made a number of concessions—more than either Luther and other hardline Protestants or the pope and conservative Catholics were likely to accept—but in the end it became obvious that the differences between the two sides were too great to be resolved through negotiation. The German prelates called again for a church council to resolve the issues, but until such a council was to meet, the humanist and curial approach to reform had hit a dead end.

Repression

Perhaps in part because of the failure of the discussions in the empire, Paul III introduced two other measures the following year (1542). The first was the Roman inquisition, designed to root out heresy and heterodoxy from the Eternal City and nearby territories. A lot of nonsense has been written about "the" inquisition (as if there were only one), so we need to set the record straight. The term *inquisition* refers broadly to a type of judicial procedure based on ancient Roman law. In an inquisitorial system, a panel of judges ran the trial. One, the investigating magistrate, looked into the facts in the case and presented it before the other judges. The judges then collectively interrogated the witnesses, examining them over and over from every conceivable angle. The assumption underlying the system was that even the most carefully crafted lie will break down if subjected to enough scrutiny. Once the evidence had all been collected, the judges made their decision. To use a modern analogy, this is similar to the way the US Supreme Court operates. In Roman law, capital cases had a very high standard of proof: either a confession or two eyewitnesses. Since eyewitnesses to capital crimes are generally hard to come by, prosecutors had to rely on confession. Particularly in cases of treason, if there was strong evidence of guilt but no confession or enough eyewitnesses, torture could be used to try to coerce a confession. With the revival of Roman law in the Middle Ages, these procedures were reintroduced in Europe. Rules were established governing the use of judicial torture, though civil governments frequently ignored them.

The inquisition in the narrower sense of a church court focused on finding and punishing heresy began in the wake of the Albigensian crusade. Without going into all the details here, Albigensianism was a religious movement centered primarily in southern France. The Catholic Church considered it heretical, though really it was more of a separate religion than a heresy. In any event, after political pressure by the church and assassinations of church officials by the Cathars, as the Albigensians were called, a crusade was called to eliminate the Albigensians altogether. Suffice it to say it worked, and hundreds of Cathars were slaughtered. To root out the remnants of the movement, the church established a court charged with finding and punishing heretics, and the inquisition was born. Other inquisitions followed whenever there was a religious movement that threatened the doctrine or power of the Catholic Church. Since heresy was considered treason against God and therefore a capital offense, if there was sufficient evidence against the accused, torture could be used to obtain a confession and a list of collaborators, following Roman law. Being fair, though, the church courts were far more likely to obey the restrictions on the use of torture than civil courts were. In Florence, for example, there are people who never even made it to the preliminary examinations in criminal cases because they died under torture before the process even began. Things like that didn't happen in church courts, though inquisitors could be pretty brutal.

The most famous inquisition, of course, was the Spanish inquisition, which began in 1478. Here again, however, there are a lot of misconceptions about the institution. The Spanish inquisition was actually controlled by the crown rather than the church. The goal of the Spanish inquisition was essentially ethnic cleansing; it was intended to make Spain a purely Christian (read "Catholic") state. The territory that became Spain had had a vibrant Jewish and Muslim culture during the Middle Ages. Many members of these communities converted to Christianity under pain of expulsion or worse during the late fifteenth century. The government suspected that these conversions were false, and that these converts were still practicing their old religions secretly. The inquisition was thus hijacked by the government to enforce its religious policies by persecuting these groups. The horrors of the Spanish inquisition, which were in all likelihood exaggerated by English propaganda, were thus ultimately the responsibility not of the church, but of the crown.

Back to the Reformation: Paul III decided in 1542 that the dangers of heresy were growing sufficiently grave, even in Rome itself, that it was time to suppress Protestantism. He thus began an inquisition in Rome, with the support of Cardinal Caraffa as inquisitor-general. Caraffa used the model of the Spanish inquisition in the new body; it had power to imprison suspects, confiscate property, and use the state to coerce confessions and inflict punishment. Paul III also supported efforts at repression in England, France, and within the empire. Caraffa later was elected pope, taking the name Paul IV (1555–1559). Paul IV continued and even intensified the work of the inquisition, even going so far as to examine Catholic reformers such as Reginald Pole for heresy. He enthusiastically supported the persecutions of Protestants by "Bloody Mary" in England and steadfastly opposed any dialogue with Protestant leaders. Curiously, he also established a ghetto in Rome on the Venetian model as an attempt to protect the Jewish community from attacks by Christians. Realizing the power of the printing press, Paul IV also established the first *Index of Prohibited Books* in an attempt to enforce censorship. It backfired; getting put on the *Index* became an easy route to best seller status, and many printers waited to see what would make the list so they would know what to print.

Paul IV's wholehearted endorsement of repression marks a clear shift away from the Catholic reformers' earlier emphasis on humanism, piety, and cleaning up abuses, and toward dogmatism, authoritarianism, and a clear Counter-Reformation emphasis within the papacy.

The Council of Trent

Paul III's final contribution toward reform was calling the long-awaited, much anticipated council of the church in 1542, the same year he started the Roman inquisition. Several matters had to be decided before the council could begin meeting and doing its work. The first was where it would meet: Paul III wanted it in Italy, since he could better control it there; Charles V wanted it in the empire, since that was where the problem started and he could better control it there. Eventually, they compromised and held the council in Trent, a city in imperial territory but on the Italian border. The council began to meet in December 1545 and continued on and off until 1563, making it the longest running council in church history. The next step was to decide whether to deal with doctrine or practice first. The Italians wanted to condemn Protestantism and delay dealing with practice since correcting abuses would inevitably have cut down on their income and perks. Charles and the Germans wanted to delay dealing with doctrine, since that would alienate Luther and his followers. Instead, they wanted to deal with abuses first so they could win the confidence of the Protestants and only later deal with theological questions. Charles was still heavily influenced by the humanist reformers, thinking the real problem was abuses. He never did understand that for the Protestants the root issue was doctrine, not practice. The council decided to take the two questions in tandem, handling alternately doctrinal and disciplinary matters.

The council's theological decisions served to reinforce and narrow traditional Catholic doctrine against Protestant challenges. Tradition was affirmed as an equal source of authority to Scripture; Protestant arguments that original sin continues to affect us after baptism were condemned; justification was declared to be not by faith alone but by works as well, following Aquinas's theology; all seven sacraments were reaffirmed, as was transubstantiation and the legitimacy of giving the laity only the bread during the Eucharist. Hubert Jedin, one of the leading historians of the council, has argued that none of these decrees marked a change in Catholic doctrine. In a sense this is correct, but as Heiko Oberman has pointed out, the decisions narrowed the scope of Catholic theology greatly by limiting the number of options considered acceptable within the church from several to just one. This narrowing of acceptable formulae in itself represents a change in doctrine. However you resolve that question, the decisions drew a line in the sand against the Protestants and defined

Catholic theology more precisely than ever before. Significantly, however, the council did not address some of the challenges the Protestants had raised against the Catholic Church, notably the power of the papacy and the doctrine of Mary. Simply put, the council was too divided to reach consensus on these questions, and thus did not address them.

In terms of disciplinary decisions, the council did much to strengthen the structure of the church. It reformed the office of bishop, revising the system for selecting bishops and ending in principle episcopal plurality (i.e., a single bishop ruling over more than one diocese) and nonresidence (i.e., a bishop living outside of his diocese)—though in the latter case exceptions could be made by papal dispensation. Bishops were made responsible for the care of all souls in their diocese and were expected to preach. They were also responsible for all decisions relating to ordination of priests in their diocese and were to see to it that priests preached in their churches as well. In what is arguably the most important disciplinary canon, the council mandated that bishops establish seminaries in each diocese, ultimately raising the quality of the clergy immeasurably across the Catholic world. The bishops were also to hold synods every three years to deal with disciplinary issues in their dioceses. In the face of challenges by secular rulers to the encroachment of church courts on such areas as marital law and probate, the council reaffirmed the authority of ecclesiastical courts in these areas.

The effects of the Council of Trent were legion. It eliminated many of the abuses in the church, strengthened the bishops, and drew a clear line between Catholic and Protestant doctrine. Together with the new religious orders, Trent contributed to a revitalized Catholicism even before the council had ended. Already in the 1540s and

'50s, a combination of church reforms and political developments in Europe meant that Catholicism was ready to attempt a comeback to regain its dominant position in European society. And it would begin where the problems had started—in the empire.

Questions for Discussion

1. In view of the information included in this chapter, how would you strike a balance between the terms "Catholic Reformation" and "Counter Reformation?"

2. The entrenched interests within the Catholic Church, such as the professional theologians and the Curia, all resisted reform, delaying the process for decades. Why do you think they did this? Was it simply a matter of corruption, or was principle involved as well?

3. Do you think a top-down or bottom-up strategy is more effective in introducing reform into large, complex institutions? What implications does your answer have for your church? For society? For government?

4. What do you think of the Jesuits' strategy of aligning themselves with the movers and shakers in society? Given that Christianity initially spread among the lower classes rather than the elites, were the Jesuits using an appropriate model for missions and political involvement? Which is more effective, grassroots activity or focusing on elites?

CHAPTER SEVEN

The Empire Strikes Back

Despite the divisions that plagued it from its earliest days, Protestantism spread rapidly across Europe. We will talk more about other countries later, but for now we need to concentrate on events in the Holy Roman Empire, where a number of the major principalities adopted "Evangelical" (i.e., Lutheran) ideas. After Saxony, the first state to convert to Lutheranism was Prussia. Prussia had been controlled by the Teutonic Knights, but when their grand master Albrecht of Hohenzollern converted to Lutheranism, the territory was secularized and the Teutonic Knights were disbanded. Philip, Landgrave of Hesse, followed suit, as did quite a number of other princes of territorial states within the empire. Many of the Imperial Free Cities also joined the Reformation, though frequently following Zwingli rather than Luther.

The Woes of Charles V

Charles V, however, believed like most rulers of his day that religious unity was essential for the survival of the state, and that Catholicism was the way to go. He could not act against the Lutherans immediately, however, because of a series of wars he was forced into. The first of these was with France, fought over rival claims to Burgundy, Milan, and southern Italy, over the fact France split the Habsburg territories in half, over the fact that the Habsburgs had France largely surrounded, over mutual rivalries from the imperial election in 1519, and so on. The first war (1521–1525) resulted in a smashing victory by Charles, who captured Francis I and forced him to sign the Treaty of Madrid (1525), renouncing claims to Milan, Genoa, and Naples and promising to return Burgundy to Charles. Francis immediately reneged when he was released, and joined by Pope Clement VII, began a second war with Charles. Charles defeated the French, and his troops sacked Rome and captured the pope in 1527 (keep that in mind—we'll see it again in the chapter on England), and forced France to sign the Peace of Cambrai (1529), which reaffirmed the terms of the Treaty of Madrid except that Charles gave up his claims to Burgundy. That same year at the Diet of Speyer, Charles tried to unite the empire to face the threat of Turkish expansion in the east. In 1526, the Turkish army had smashed the Hungarian army and crusading forces at the battle of Mohacs, and this threatened to open the way to Vienna to the Ottoman forces. Charles, however, insisted that the Lutheran princes submit to his authority in matters of religion, prompting a number of them to respond with a protestation, from which we get the word *Protestant,* in which they refused to compromise their religious beliefs.

The next year (1530), the ever hopeful Charles presided personally over the Diet of Augsburg, thinking that if the leaders of the two sides would just sit down and talk, the whole thing could be resolved. Luther was still under the imperial ban, so Melanchthon presented a very moderate statement of beliefs known as the Augsburg Confession. It was written to please the emperor and in the hopes that some kind of compromise might be reached—though it refused to budge on certain key points. Unfortunately, the papal representatives wouldn't give an inch on their key issues in dispute, including papal supremacy, the nature of the priesthood, the Mass, and the importance of merit and works in salvation. So the Augsburg Confession actually served to cement the split between the two churches.

Anticipating war, the Protestant princes promptly prepared a defensive alliance to resist the emperor. And then they hit a snag: Luther refused to support them. Following his reading of Romans 13, Luther insisted that subjects needed to obey the governing powers, and since the emperor was the highest governing power in the empire, the princes had no right to oppose him actively; passive resistance was fine, but nothing more. It is a bit awkward to go to war to support a religious movement whose leader does not agree with you, so the princes decided they needed to take drastic action: They sent in the lawyers. The lawyers' argument was that in the general case Luther was right, but he did not take into account the peculiarities of the Holy Roman Empire. Since the emperor was elected, he was answerable to the electors in certain specific ways.

Should he do something illegal or break his word, it was not only the right but the duty of the electors to oppose him. Private citizens did not have this right, but the "inferior" or "lesser" magistrates, who are themselves part of the "powers that be" from Romans 13, could lead in active resistance in the specific context of imperial law. Luther reluctantly agreed, and in the Torgau Memorandum of 1530, declared that *if* the lawyers were right, *if* the lesser magistrates had the duty to resist unjust commands from the emperor, and *if* the emperor did something unjust, then the princes could take part in active resistance against Charles. That was all it took. In 1531, eight of the Lutheran princes and representatives of eleven of the Imperial Free Cities met in Schmalkalden to draw up a mutual defense pact known as the Schmalkaldic League to resist imperial efforts to re-Catholicize them.

Things might have come quickly to blows, but the Turks under Suleiman the Magnificient (1520–1566) were starting to get frisky again and were actually approaching Vienna. So Charles set up a truce with the Protestants in 1532, granting them religious toleration until the two sides could iron out their differences, and with Protestant support he led an army to relieve Vienna. The Ottomans withdrew, but at the same time there was a coordinated Arab, Barbary, and Turkish attack on the Mediterranean coasts of Italy and Spain. Charles went to deal with that, but after some successes received word that the French had allied themselves with the Turks and planned to attack his back while he was occupied in the Mediterranean. Francis I had decided to go after Milan when the Sforza dynasty there died out. Charles was forced to send troops to outflank the French as they marched through Savoy; he also attacked from the Low Countries. The situation resulted in a stalemate, so in 1538 a peace agreement was reached. Charles was no dummy, though, and must have known that Francis was likely to break it at the first opportunity.

Charles then turned his attentions back to religious affairs in the empire. He hoped that the series of colloquies held in 1540–1541 would settle matters, but as we saw in chapter 6, they failed. He did get one important break from an unlikely source, however: Philip of Hesse, one of the anchors of the Schmalkaldic League. Philip had been married at nineteen to the daughter of Duke George of Saxony, the sponsor of the Leipzig Debate. After a while, he began to bemoan the fact that he couldn't maintain a normal sex life with her, and as a result adopted a grossly immoral lifestyle until he came under the influence of Luther. He had fallen madly in lust with a young woman at court named Margaret von der Saal. He began to lobby Luther, Melanchthon, Bucer, and just about anyone else who he thought might help to allow him to enter a bigamous marriage with her, on the grounds that bigamy—following the example of the biblical patriarchs—was a less serious sin than either adultery or divorce, an idea he got from Luther's "Babylonian Captivity." (As an aside, this seems to have been Clement VII's preferred solution to Henry VIII's request for an annulment from Catherine of Aragon, on the advice of Cardinal Cajetan.) Luther rather reluctantly agreed, on the condition that Philip keep the bigamous marriage secret, so in 1540 Philip married Margaret, apparently with the agreement of his first wife. Unfortunately, he didn't keep his mouth shut, and Charles got wind of it. At about this point, Cleves, an anti-Habsburg Protestant duchy just east of imperial possessions in the Low Countries, was looking to join the Schmalkaldic League. Due to a combination of dynastic inheritances and alliances with France and England (through the marriage of the duke's daughter Anne to Henry VIII), Cleves was an

emerging regional power. Charles, however, had claims on the duchy, and he certainly didn't want it allied with France. So he pressured Philip into opposing Cleves's entrance into the Schmalkaldic League; in return, Charles wouldn't bring Philip down on bigamy charges and would advance him in the imperial service. Philip's son-in-law Maurice, duke of Saxony, was brought in on the deal, as was Joachim II of Brandenburg, who was allowed to control his church in roughly the same way Henry VIII in England did. The net result is that Philip's bigamy provided the wedge that allowed Charles to split the Schmalkaldic League, as well as embarrassing the Protestant reformers and producing a lot of animosity between the Protestant princes.

Charles still couldn't act against the Protestants, however, because he found himself at war again. The French had again allied themselves with the Turks, and their combined fleets were pillaging Spain and Italy. At the same time, Francis also launched an invasion of the Low Countries, and Suleiman was advancing in the Danube valley. Charles let his brother defend Austria and ignored the Mediterranean as well. Instead, Charles allied himself with Henry VIII of England, seized Cleves, and with Henry's help invaded France. Charles did well enough that Francis was forced to sign the Peace of Crépy (1544), ending the Habsburg-Valois wars. Shortly thereafter Charles signed an armistice with the Turks, and he once again turned to the religious question within the empire.

The First Schmalkaldic War

The Council of Trent began to meet in 1545; the Lutherans who attended were in no mood to compromise, and Paul III was equally convinced that the best thing to do would be to crush them like a bug. Luther, who had worked hard to avoid religious war in Germany, died in 1546. That same year Charles refused to renew the terms allowing for religious toleration for Lutherans, and it became obvious that it was only a matter of time before war broke out. To prepare for the war, Charles did his best to detach as many Protestant princes from the Schmalkaldic League as possible. In particular, he promised Maurice of Ducal Saxony the office of elector instead of his rival John Frederick of Electoral Saxony, plus several cities and freedom from any anti-Protestant provisions passed by Trent in return for Maurice's support. Since Charles had so many Protestants on his side—a fact which must have galled him since his entire policy was based on the necessity of religious unity—he began looking for legal as opposed to religious grounds for attacking the remaining Protestant princes. Charles seems to have realized that the conflict was not simply about religion but involved territorialism and nationalism against the medieval concept of empire, so he used legal and political issues to justify his mobilization. The war broke out in 1546. The Schmalkaldic League initially had more troops and a very able commander, but every decision had to be made by a dithering council of war, giving Charles time to expand his army. John Frederick of Electoral Saxony had so much success against Charles's brother Ferdinand and against Maurice, who had been made elector in October of 1546, that Charles had to move his forces north to deal with him. At the battle of Mühlberg in April 1547, Charles's army, led by Fernando Alvarez de Toledo, duke of Alva, won a smashing victory against the Schmalkaldic League. Charles captured John Frederick; Maurice had promised that Philip of Hesse would be treated leniently, but when he presented himself to Charles he was imprisoned as well.

The Interims

Charles seemed to have won all the marbles. The Schmalkaldic League was defeated and its leaders imprisoned, Cologne was forcibly re-Catholicized, and nearly all the cities in Germany submitted to Charles's authority, with the notable exceptions of Bremen and Magdeburg. He did face a number of problems, however, and not all of them had to do with the Protestants. The pope wanted to use Trent to strengthen the papacy and condemn the Protestants; Charles wanted to settle the differences with the

Protestants through dialogue (or through a German church council if necessary) and to reform the papacy. The council, fearing pressure from Charles, withdrew to Bologna, and Charles declared the decrees null and void until they returned to Trent. Meanwhile, he had to figure out how to deal with the religious situation in Germany. His first attempt, known as the Augsburg Interim (1548), was drawn up by theologians representing different groups in the empire. It was essentially Catholic, but it grafted on some concessions to the Protestants, such as clerical marriage with papal dispensation, Communion in both kinds, and a modified restatement of the doctrine of justification by faith (which had just been repudiated by Trent). It was to be binding on Catholics and Protestants alike, and no one really liked it. Some territories accepted it formally, but no one put it into practice. Elector Maurice, whose territories now included the Lutheran heartland, couldn't enforce it, so the bishop of Naumburg worked with Melanchthon on a further compromise known as the Leipzig Interim (also 1548), which was essentially Lutheran with some Catholic influences, including the use of the Latin Mass, celebration of Catholic fasts and feasts, and recognition of all seven sacraments. Although the Leipzig Interim replaced the Augsburg Interim in many places, it still met with only limited acceptance, especially in the north, which openly defied Charles's religious policies. The northern cities, led by Magdeburg, essentially told the emperor that he would need to send his army and reduce them one by one if he wanted to enforce his religious policies, because they were not going to budge.

To make matters worse, Charles was also facing political problems. The princes didn't like his treatment of John Frederick and Philip of Hesse, nor did they like his attempts to force them to appoint his son Philip Habsburg (the future Philip II of Spain) as his successor—a move which led to a temporary split between Charles and his brother Ferdinand as well. Further, the Turks were again threatening to move up the Danube valley, and Henri II of France had concluded a peace treaty with England, which itself was providing a haven for Protestant refugees from the empire, making another war with France and the Turks look inevitable. At this point (1550), several Protestant princes began forming a resurgent Schmalkaldic League, building not only on the religious issues but on a nationalistic resentment of the Spanish troops Charles had brought in to try to enforce the Leipzig Interim. Even Maurice of Saxony, annoyed at Charles for his treatment of his father-in-law Philip of Hesse and having already achieved his goal of becoming the Saxon elector, also joined the renewed Schmalkaldic League. The league then made an alliance with Henri II, offering him the title of "imperial vicar" of Metz, Toul, and Verdun in return for financial support against Charles, making this the first of many territorial sacrifices that would be made on the altar of local interests over the interests of the empire.

The Second Schmalkaldic War and the Religious Peace of Augsburg

War broke out quickly. Henri II reasserted France's claim on Flanders, Milan, and Naples and sent 35,000 troops into Lorraine. In the meantime, the Protestant princes gathered another 35,000 men in Franconia. Charles wasn't ready to face such numbers and was uncertain of his brother Ferdinand's loyalty, so he fled. Despite this, many of the Imperial Free Cities continued to support Charles; evidently, they feared the princes more than the emperor. Strasbourg also held off the French army, and Margrave

Albert Alcibiades, one of the Protestant princes, decided it would be more profitable to plunder Franconia and create his own duchy out of Würzburg and Bamberg, and so dropped out of the coalition. The Protestants thus did not have as smooth a time as they had hoped, and Maurice was forced to negotiate with Ferdinand. The two reached a tentative settlement in August 1552, which resulted in the release of Philip of Hesse from prison (John Frederick having been released earlier) and toleration for Lutherans until the next diet, which was to settle the religious question. Charles then allied himself with Alcibiades in a failed attempt to drive the French from Metz, after which Charles abandoned the empire altogether, leaving matters in his brother's hands. Alcibiades went back to plundering Franconia. Ferdinand and Maurice campaigned together against the Turks in Hungary for a time, after which Maurice attacked Alcibiades in an attempt to restore order in the empire. Maurice's forces defeated Alcibiades, but Maurice himself died in the battle at age thirty-two (1553). Order was finally restored in 1554, when Alcibiades was decisively defeated and fled to France.

The diet finally met in Augsburg in 1555 from February to August. The emperor was not present, nor was any meaningful papal representative, since Julius III died in March and his successor Marcellus II, chosen in April, died in May. By the time the next pope, Paul IV (Caraffa) had been elected and had decided what to do in Germany, the summer and the diet were nearly over. The electors and most of the princes were also missing in action. The remaining princes took the lead in the negotiations, however, and after many compromises, the terms of the Religious Peace of Augsburg were hammered out. The Lutheran princes, imperial knights, and Imperial Free Cities were guaranteed security equal to the Catholic states; each state could decide whether it was Catholic or Lutheran following the principle later codified as *cuius regio, eius religio* ("to whom the rule, his the religion")— that is, each ruler had the right to decide which religion would be followed in her/his/their territory; ecclesiastical states ruled by an abbot, bishop, or archbishop could not convert to Lutheranism—if the ruler himself converted, he had to abdicate; and finally, in a secret provision, Catholic ecclesiastical territories would tolerate adherents of the Augsburg Confession.

Two things are worth noting about the Religious Peace of Augsburg. First, the only acceptable affiliations were Lutheran or Catholic; there was no provision for tolerating Calvinists—a dynamic, rapidly growing branch of Protestantism in the 1550s—nor Anabaptists or any other group. This was a glaring example of the divisions within the Protestant world, one which would have ominous results in the Thirty Years' War. Second, once again it is clear that for the princes, local and territorial authority mattered far more than the empire. By the beginning of the next century, religious warfare would be one of the catalysts for a growing trend toward centralization in government known as absolutism and a countertrend toward strict limitations on rulers known as constitutionalism. But even in the mid-1550s, lines were already being drawn between an anti-Habsburg nationalistic and territorial focus, and an imperial conception with roots in the medieval empire but moving more and more toward absolutism. This too would be a contributing factor to the Thirty Years' War.

As for Charles, sadly, he finally got it: The religious question was not one that could be settled by cleaning up abuses and discussion among religious leaders. His humanistic, liberal Catholic approach was a failure. He was so despondent over his inability to enforce religious unity

within his territories that he decided enough was enough. In 1556, he abdicated, giving his brother Ferdinand his territories in Austria, and his son Philip his territories in the Low Countries, Spain, and the Spanish possessions in Italy as well as in Africa and the New World. He retired to a villa in Spain and died in September 1558.

Patching Up Lutheranism

The Religious Peace of Augsburg left a religiously divided empire in its wake, but the Schmalkaldic wars also left a divided Lutheranism. The two principal factions were the moderate Philippists, supporters of Melanchthon who had been willing to compromise at least to some extent with the Catholics during the Interims, and the Gnesio-Lutherans, the hardliners who had held out against the emperor and in the end forced the concessions given in the Religious Peace of Augsburg. Theological differences also divided the two. The Philippists argued that free will was involved to some extent in salvation, and that some good works helped the process along. Some went further, becoming "Cryptocalvinists" and adopting some of Calvin's ideas on the relationship of works and salvation. The Gnesio-Lutherans held to a strict interpretation of *sola gratia* and *sola fide*, denying works any role in salvation at all. There were divisions over which version of the Augsburg Confession should be adopted, the 1530 or the 1540 (known as the *Variata*). Ultimately, a middle group would develop in the universities in Leipzig, Rostock, Marburg, and Tübingen. Led by Jakob Andreae, these theologians worked to preserve Lutheranism by steering a middle road between the extremes. In 1575, the churches of Swabia and Lower Saxony accepted a set of articles written by Andreae. Over the next five years, this would be further developed into the *Book of Concord* (1580), which would ultimately unite most Lutherans and formally end the divisions between the Gnesio-Lutherans and the Philippists.

Although Lutheranism continued to play a major role within the empire and in Scandinavia, its influence outside Germanic territories was declining. In its place, Calvinism had emerged as the most dynamic and influential force within the Protestant world. We turn now to the man and the movement he started.

Questions for Discussion

1. Charles V believed that it was impossible to hold a religiously divided empire together. Do you think countries need a common set of beliefs to remain united? In the absence of a core set of beliefs, can a society hold together, or will centrifugal forces tear it apart? Why or why not?

2. In view of France's alliance with the Turks, how do you

weigh the relative role of religion versus dynastic politics to the French king? How do you explain Henri II's persecution of Protestants at home (see chapter 12) while supporting the Turks against a Catholic monarch?

3. How would you have handled Philip of Hesse's request? Can you identify any parallels today in which we are asked to compromise our morality or our beliefs for political, economic, or social support?

4. How do you account for the Lutheran Maurice of Saxony's support of the emperor against his fellow Protestants in the Schmalkaldic League, then his change in allegiance during the Interims? What is the role of religion versus politics in his decisions? (Remember, he remained Lutheran and protected the church in his home territory throughout the period.)

5. Who do you think was more faithful to Luther's vision, the Philippists or the Gnesio-Lutherans? Why?

CHAPTER EIGHT

John Calvin: Biography

We turn now to John Calvin, by most measures the most important theologian of the Protestant Reformation. Calvin was born on July 10, 1509, in the city of Noyon in Picardy, France, close to the Belgian border. He came from a solidly middle-class family; his father was a notary (sort of a JV lawyer who drafted legal documents, witnessed contracts, etc., in an era of widespread illiteracy) who did a great deal of business with the bishop of Noyon. The bishop sponsored a school for his family, and the elder Calvin's connections with the bishop meant that John was one of only a few students unrelated to the bishop who attended this school. When John completed grammar school, his father arranged for the bishop to give him a benefice to finance his higher education, and so John was named priest of a village in the diocese of Noyons. He wasn't ordained, of course, and in any event was too young to become a priest legally. But he was nonetheless entitled to collect the revenues from the village, out of which he paid a priest to act as his vicar in the village—that is, to say Mass, baptize, marry, hold funerals, and so forth. The difference between the revenues and the vicar's salary paid John's college expenses. This was pretty much standard procedure for people attending college in late medieval and early modern Europe. Students were considered part of the clergy anyway, so you could think of the benefice as a kind of scholarship. His father intended for him to study theology; normally, canon (i.e., church) law would have been a better choice for advancing to high office in the church, but in 1521 with Luther and Protestantism getting rolling, theology looked like a growth industry and must have seemed a better bet.

At age twelve, John left Noyons for the University of Paris. The university was made up of a number of residential colleges, much like they still have at Oxford, for example. Students lived and took classes in a single building or complex. All students studied the liberal arts until they received a bachelor's degree, after which they could pursue advanced training in liberal arts or in one of the "higher" faculties of law, medicine, or theology. Calvin started off at the Collège de la Marche, but quickly transferred to the Collège Montaigu. This was an absolutely first-rate school: strict, hard nosed, and academically rigorous. To put it in perspective, consider that Erasmus had attended here for a time, and Calvin, Ignatius Loyola (the founder of the Jesuits), and Rabelais (the brilliant French burlesque novelist) all completed their degrees at Montaigu. All moved in radically different directions, but they were also all marked by their experiences at the school.

Once John completed his BA, he prepared to move on to advanced study. Unfortunately, however, John's father had a falling out with the bishop and decided that the clergy were all a bunch of no-good scum. Since M. Calvin didn't want his son in such a sleazy profession, he decided John should become a lawyer instead. So John enrolled in the law program at Orléans under Pierre de L'Estoile. French legal scholarship at this time was heavily influenced by humanism, and from his first exposure to it at Orléans John was hooked. He left Orléans for Bourges, pursuing the most advanced humanist legal training he could find. Calvin probably met his first Protestant here (Melchior Wolmar, his Greek professor) in the course of completing his law degree.

In 1531, John's father died, freeing John to pursue a career in humanism rather than law. He returned to Paris to do postdoctoral work at the Collège Fortet, a school known for its flexible curriculum, academic freedom, and humanistic focus. He also attended the royal lectures founded by Francis I to promote humanistic studies within France. French humanism was a bit different in some respects from humanism elsewhere in Europe. Rather than focusing almost exclusively on classical scholarship, French humanists tended to push programs for reforming society, including the church. One of the most important early humanists in France was Guillaume Budé, a legal scholar who specialized in the Greek text of the Roman law code. (Yes, Greek, not Latin; the main compilation of Roman law was done by Justinian I, the Byzantine emperor, and was in Greek.) Budé was living in Paris, and when Calvin returned the two became close friends. In fact, after Budé's death, the rest of the family converted to Protestantism and moved to Geneva under Calvin's sponsorship.

Calvin Becomes a Protestant

During this stay in Paris, Calvin also developed an interest in church reform, though he was not yet a Protestant. In fact, his first published work, a commentary on Seneca's *De Clementia* ("On Mercy"), shows no trace of Protestant influence. Seneca was an ancient Stoic, a member of a school of philosophy that had a view of morality similar to that of Christianity. As a result, the stoics were very popular among Renaissance humanists. Erasmus had written a commentary on *De Clementia* some time before Calvin did. Following the time-honored practice of scholars, Calvin decided to build his reputation by climbing over the bodies of his predecessors, and thus decided he needed to "correct" some of Erasmus's (mis)interpretations. This work was published in 1532, indicating that Calvin was an orthodox, if somewhat progressive, Catholic at this time.

The situation was quite a bit different in 1533, however. One of Calvin's friends, Nicholas Cop, had been named rector of the University of Paris. In his inaugural address, he presented an essentially Erasmian interpretation of the Sermon on the Mount. But he coupled this with a contrast between the "new" and "old" religion that sounded suspiciously Protestant, especially when combined with the impassioned tone of the speech. When word got out, the authorities instituted a search for Cop *and Calvin,* who both decided it would be a good idea to leave the city, since Protestants had been burned to death by the authorities in Paris not long before this. Calvin was included in the warrant because there was some suspicion that he had ghostwritten the speech. Historians have not established whether he did or not, although a copy of the speech in Calvin's own handwriting does survive. Whether or not he wrote the speech, however, Calvin did adopt Protestant ideas sometime during 1533, though when exactly is unclear. He suggests in his Psalms commentary that he experienced a sudden conversion; perhaps when he saw the backlash against the modest, Erasmian-style reforms in Cop's speech, he decided that a more radical, thoroughgoing reform was necessary. On the other hand, his conversion may have been before the Cop affair and influenced the tone of the address. Calvin's relative reticence about details of his personal life makes it quite difficult to work out some critical elements of his biography.

When Calvin left Paris, he traveled quite a bit. He visited Angoulême, where he met Lefèvre d'Etaples, who was living under the protection of Marguerite, the sister of King Francis I. Lefèvre was a humanist reformer whose commentary on the book of Romans, published in 1512, five years *before* the Ninety-five Theses, argued for justification by faith alone, supposedly the distinctive doctrine of Luther. Calvin also went to Poitiers, Orléans, Strasbourg, Basel, and other cities. During this time, several important events occurred in Calvin's life. In 1534 he resigned his benefices; that same year he also wrote his first theological work, the *Psychopannychia,* an attack on the doctrine of soul sleep (that is, that after death our souls go to sleep until the Last Judgment) that was published in 1542. Most importantly, however, in 1535 he settled in the city of Basel to study theology using books produced by the city's presses. Most of these were editions of early Christian writers, especially Augustine, but also Cyprian and Tertullian; he also read lots of Luther and some Bucer and Oecolampadius (the reformer of Basel), a few Catholic authors such as Peter Lombard and Gratian (who compiled the basic text of church law), and lots of Bible in Greek and Hebrew. This reading provided Calvin with his theological education. In other words, Calvin was a self-taught theologian, a remarkable feat particularly in view of his subsequent career. After a year of study, Calvin produced the first edition of his most important work, the *Institutes of the Christian Religion*. This edition was relatively short, a few hundred pages in a modern English translation. But for the rest of Calvin's career, he would expand it, answer challenges, and elaborate it, so that the text of the final versions (1559 in Latin, 1560 in French) in modern editions numbers 1500 pages. The *Institutes* is often misunderstood, as if anything Calvin had to say could be found in it. In fact, the *Institutes* was designed to deal with subjects that could be found throughout Scripture. Calvin decided to put them in one place so that when he wrote his commentaries, he wouldn't have to keep repeating the material and could focus instead on what was unique to the passage itself. Calvin became an instant sensation in the Protestant world because of this book, which would become the most important work of the Protestant Reformation and one of its first systematic theologies.

After publishing the *Institutes,* Calvin spent some time in Ferrara, where he got to know the Duchess Renée, a

protector of a number of Protestant thinkers. The two carried on an extensive correspondence for years afterward, with Calvin acting as an advisor to the duchess. From there he returned to France to settle some issues related to his estate and to convince his brother Antoine and his wife Marie to join him. He intended to return to Basel or perhaps Strasbourg, but a minor matter of a war forced him into a fateful detour to the city of Geneva.

Farel and Calvin

Before we look at Calvin's first stay in Geneva, we need to back up and look at the history of the city itself. Up until 1536, Geneva was an episcopal city, that is, it was legally under the authority of its bishop, who was also a prince within the Holy Roman Empire. The bishop, however, was usually in attendance at the imperial court, so he left the city in the hands of a vicar-general—his official representative—and the canons of the cathedral. (Technically, a cathedral is simply the principal church of a bishop, where he has his seat—Latin, *cathedra,* "throne." The canons were the big guns of the cathedral, the priests who elected the bishop and called most of the shots within the local church.) In terms of power politics, since it was part of the empire, the city was not part of the Swiss Confederacy. The bishop tended to ally himself with the duke of Savoy (i.e., the region including northwestern Italy and southeastern France), who often had more say about what happened in Geneva than the bishop himself. Given a chance, the duke would have liked to annex Geneva. Sometimes, however, the bishop would ally himself with the king of France, who was generally a rival of the duke of Savoy.

Day-to-day affairs in the city were actually run by the Small Council, a group of laymen elected from the upper segments of the population. The Small Council resented the domination of Savoy and was also rather put out by their nonresident bishop. These political tensions were magnified by religious dissatisfaction in the city. Literate lay people began reading the Bible, now available thanks to printing, and began to publicly challenge preachers about their teaching: "But what you're saying contradicts the Bible! I just read in the Gospel of Matthew that . . . How does what you're saying fit in with that?" With Catholic preachers being shouted down by their congregations, the Small Council decided it was time to act. In 1536 the Small Council booted out the bishop, the duke's representatives, the priests, monks, nuns—about two hundred to three hundred clergy, plus their support staff of about a thousand people, totaling roughly 10 percent of the city's population. The Small Council then set up an alliance with the militarily powerful canton of Bern. In return for military protection, Bern wanted to see Geneva move toward Protestantism, so it paid for preachers to reform the city. The most important of these was Guillaume Farel, a fiery French preacher who had worked with Lefèvre d'Etaples at Meaux (see chapter 12) and had since become a convinced Protestant. Under his preaching, Geneva officially joined the Reformed Protestant camp.

In the middle of all of this turmoil, Calvin arrived in Geneva—the same year that his *Institutes* had been published. Word soon reached Farel that Calvin was in the city. Farel hurried to the inn where Calvin was staying and immediately began a full-court press to convince him to stay. Farel told Calvin that he was not there by accident, that it had instead been God's providence that brought him to Geneva to help reform the city. Calvin told Farel that he had no interest in becoming a pastor; he was a scholar and wanted to be left alone to study and write, and that by doing so he could do the cause of the gospel far more good than if he were saddled with the day-to-day affairs of running a church. Farel told him he was being stubborn and was resisting God's call to him. Calvin replied that he thought God was calling him to scholarship. Finally, Farel told Calvin that God was calling him to Geneva, and if he refused to stay he would be guilty of rejecting God's call and God would get him for it. This shook Calvin up enough that he rather reluctantly decided to stay and help Farel.

Oddly enough, however, Calvin was not hired as a pastor. Instead, his primary job was as a "doctor," that is, a teacher. He gave regular lectures on the Bible and theology, and assisted Farel in establishing a church order for the city. Unfortunately, Calvin and Farel had a falling-out with the Small Council in 1538 over the issue of church discipline. They insisted that the church had the right to excommunicate unrepentant sinners without interference from the state; the Small Council insisted it had the right to lift sentences of excommunication even without the pastors' approval. Calvin and Farel finally delivered an ultimatum: If an excommunicated person presented herself or himself for Communion with the approval of the Small Council, they would refuse to celebrate Communion at all. The Small Council responded by firing Farel and Calvin and kicking them out of the city.

Farel returned to Bern, where he settled in Neuchâtel in the recently conquered French-speaking part of the canton. Calvin continued to his original destination, the city of Strasbourg, where he was named pastor of the French refugee church in the city under the supervision of its great reformer, Martin Bucer.

Calvin and Bucer

Martin Bucer was an ex-Dominican theologian who had become a Protestant in the earliest days of the Reformation. He had participated in the Marburg Colloquy on Zwingli's side, although Bucer always considered himself a follower of Luther. Unlike any other significant figure of his day, Bucer worked tirelessly for reconciliation within the church, between Luther and Zwingli, Evangelical and Reformed, even Protestant and Catholic. In his capacity as de facto head of the Strasbourg church, Bucer worked closely with the young Calvin once he became pastor of the French refugee church in the city. Among other things, the two attended a number of conferences with other Protestant and Catholic leaders to try to settle some of the rifts caused by the Protestant Reformation. In one of these meetings in 1539, he met and became friends with Philip Melanchthon, Luther's protégé at Wittenberg. Melanchthon then encouraged Bucer to send Calvin to Regensburg in 1541 to meet with Protestant and Catholic leaders to try to reach some compromise that could reconcile the two sides. (As we have seen, the meeting was a failure; although moderates agreed to a formula to try to bring the sides together, hardliners on both sides—including Calvin—refused to go along with it.) Perhaps most importantly, by working with Bucer at these conferences, Calvin learned to temper his abrasive personality and to be more diplomatic in his approach to people. Although still a type double-A personality, Calvin did manage to soften his style a bit because of these experiences.

Calvin's theology, especially in the area of ecclesiology (i.e., the doctrine of the church), also underwent important developments in this time. Bucer's ideas on church structure and organization transformed Calvin's thinking in these areas and laid the foundation for his later work on church order, arguably his most important contribution to Christian thought. Ultimately, the Reformed and Presbyterian churches in western Europe based their local church organization on the model Calvin would draw up in 1541 for Geneva, which in turn was based on Bucer's ecclesiastical principles passed on to Calvin during his stay in Strasbourg. We will talk more about that church structure in the next chapter.

Another important event of Calvin's Strasbourg period was his marriage. Given the Catholic practice of clerical celibacy, most Protestant reformers insisted that pastors get married. Unmarried pastors looked too much like Catholic priests to an unsophisticated laity and thus gave the wrong impression of the pastors' allegiance. So Bucer told Calvin he needed to get married. Calvin didn't want to bother; he had enough work to do without taking the time to go wooing some woman. Bucer insisted, however, so Calvin, ever the romantic Frenchman, thought up a compromise. He drew up a list of qualifications for a wife, told Bucer to screen potential candidates, and then promised to interview them and pick one. There were actually two lists of qualifications, one public, one private. The public list included things such as godliness, good household management skills, and some concern for Calvin's health (this was no joke—he was already beginning to develop some of the debilitating illnesses that would plague him for the rest of his rather short life). The private list specified that she have a pleasant personality and things of that sort. The lists were drawn up and candidates were selected, but Calvin jumped the list and married Idelette du Bure, the widow of an Anabaptist. Despite what we would consider an unpromising start, the two were very happy together. Unfortunately, however, in 1542 Idelette gave birth prematurely to a baby boy, who died shortly thereafter. Her health was ruined by the experience, and she died herself in 1549. Calvin never remarried, not because he'd "been there, done that" and no longer had anything to prove, but because to the day he died he never stopped mourning the loss of Idelette.

As an aside, it is worth noting that early in the Reformation, Luther and his compatriots closed the monasteries and convents around Wittenberg (with the approval of the Elector) and encouraged those inside to get married. In at least one case, a number of nuns snuck out of their convent hidden in barrels before it was shut down. After two years, only one of these nuns, Katherine von Bora, was unmarried or had not returned to her family. She was apparently not very attractive, and at twenty-six was too old for marriage anyway. Luther attempted to do some matchmaking, first with a student, then with another minister whom she rejected; she then offered to marry either Luther or another theology professor. Luther couldn't think of any reason not to, so he married her on June 13, 1525. The Luthers, too, had a wonderful relationship, and Luther often referred to his wife as "Katie my rib." I can't prove this, but personally, I suspect Katie was gunning for Luther from day one. I think she knew she wanted to marry him and just bided her time until the opportunity arose. This is just a suspicion, mind you, but from what I know about Katie, I wouldn't put it past her.

Calvin's stay in Strasbourg was the happiest period of his life and a critical one for his formation as a theologian and pastor. Unfortunately, at least from his perspective, it only lasted a few years, from 1538 to 1541. Events would lead him back to Geneva, where he would live for the rest of his life.

The Return to Geneva

While Calvin was in Strasbourg, Geneva found itself under increasing pressure to return to Catholicism. This came from several directions: from the bishop, who wanted his city back; from the duke of Savoy, who wanted to see his influence over the city restored; and from Jacopo Sadoletto, a highly trained humanist and cardinal in the Catholic Church who challenged Protestant doctrine and appealed to the populace to return to the Catholic fold. Sadoletto sent a letter to Geneva, using all of his impressive powers of persuasion and erudition to show Genevans the error of their ways in straying from the One True Church and inviting them back into fellowship with Rome. In 1536, a combination of political self-interest and popular religious feeling had led to a break with the bishop and with Rome. Now, with the first flush of the Reformation past, the same combination of political and religious pressures threatened to sink the reformation into the Rhone.

With Calvin and Farel gone, Geneva had no theologians who could counter Sadoletto's letter, and the Small Council had to face the real danger that they might lose control of the city to the bishop unless they could find someone who could help them. The first person they thought of was Calvin. They sent a letter to him in Strasbourg, admitting that they had not parted on the best of terms, but appealing to him to help anyway since there was a real danger that Geneva would be lost to Protestantism if Sadoletto's letter went unanswered. Calvin rather reluctantly agreed to help. He wrote a powerful reply to the cardinal's letter that shredded its arguments so completely that the Genevan Reformation was definitively saved. The Small Council was so grateful that it invited him to return to take over the reins of the reform in the city.

Calvin was less than pleased with the invitation. His memories of Geneva were hardly positive, and his exile from the city still rankled. Besides, he genuinely loved Strasbourg. So he turned the Small Council down flat. The Small Council asked him what it would take to convince him to return. Calvin laid out his conditions: He wanted a large house near the church, a reasonably generous salary, and so forth. (Incidentally, his salary included five hundred liters of wine annually, roughly two bottles a day. He was, after all, French. To be fair, this was intended to supply some of the needs of his household.) But in addition to the normal sorts of issues one would think of when negotiating for a new position, Calvin also demanded a free hand to organize the church as he saw fit without interference from the government, the very issue that had led to his exile in the first place. Much to Calvin's surprise, the city agreed to all of his terms. With more than

a little regret, Calvin decided that since the Small Council had met his demands, he was duty-bound to return to Geneva. And so he left Strasbourg to return to the city that had kicked him out three years before.

Calvin was now given a new job in Geneva: He was named one of the city's pastors, while continuing as a "doctor" (i.e., theology teacher) as well. In fact, when he returned to Geneva one of his first public acts was to teach a Bible class. He walked into the room and said, "When we last met, we discussed such and such a verse; we now go on to the next." He then continued as if there had not been a three-year hiatus in his lectures. Every now and then, the man certainly showed style. He also drafted the *Ecclesiastical Ordinances* for the city of Geneva, laying out the complete structure of the church, a structure we will examine in the next chapter. But along with this, he performed some very important functions in the civil government. As the most highly trained lawyer in the city, he drafted and helped interpret the city's civil ordinances. It is worth noting that this law code was designed to keep the church from interfering in state affairs as much as possible, and vice versa. Contrary to the way Calvin's Geneva is usually described, he had no intention of developing a theocracy or of having the church dominate the state. Among other things, the government would never have stood for it; the city went Protestant in the first place in an effort to end ecclesiastical control over the city. In addition to his role in drafting the city's constitution, Calvin's legal training also made him a consultant to the Small Council on ecclesiastical, civil, and diplomatic matters.

Geneva as a City of Refuge

Once Calvin returned to Geneva, increasing numbers of refugees fleeing religious persecution arrived in the city.

Calvin's growing reputation as a theologian was undoubtedly one reason for this, but there were a number of other less obvious ones as well. Because of the political and religious situation in the Holy Roman Empire, only people who held to the Lutheran view of the Lord's Supper could settle in its Protestant cities and principalities. But this view of the Supper was rejected by virtually every significant reformer outside of Germany, and so religious refugees were generally unwelcome there. Calvin's openness to refugees and his more congenial view of the Supper enabled many more to go to Geneva, including significant numbers from England and Scotland. Another factor was geography: Geneva is on the borders of both France and Italy, and was thus a relatively convenient place for refugees from these countries to go to. Further, although the principal language was Savoyard, a cross between French and Italian, Calvin was a native speaker of French and preached in French. This made the city a particularly desirable place to be for French Protestants, and all the more so since in the 1540s Calvin became the first person to publish significant theological works in French. This helped determine the theological direction of the growing Protestant movement in the kingdom (see chapter 12) and attracted Huguenot leaders to Geneva.

As a result, the overwhelming number of refugees in Geneva came from France, so much so that French increasingly replaced Savoyard as the main language on the streets. And as is the case historically, these refugees most often came from relatively affluent groups rather than the poor; they had the money and the connections to make it out during hard times, while the poor had to stay behind. Thus, not only were the French beginning to outnumber the native Genevans, but their wealth bought them a great deal of influence in the city. Not surprisingly, many

Genevans were unhappy with this situation. An organization called the Sons of Geneva formed as an anti-French (and therefore anti-Calvin) faction within the city. This was a risky move; factions were considered very dangerous in early modern republics, so much so that most even banned political parties. (This view carried over into the US Constitution, which made no provisions for political parties and was generally hostile to them.) But the Genevans felt so strongly that they were being marginalized in their own city that they believed they had to do something. The leader of the Sons of Geneva was Ami Perrin, a prominent citizen who had been one of Calvin's main supporters in the city during his exile; in fact, he was a leader in the drive to bring Calvin back in 1541. But the direction the city took in the years following Calvin's return disturbed Perrin. The question of French influence was only one factor in Perrin's disillusionment. The consistory, a church court set up by Calvin (which will be discussed in the next chapter), censured members of Perrin's family, which also soured him on the way Geneva was being run. Suffice it to say that Perrin emerged as the leader of the anti-French faction, which challenged Calvin's influence in Geneva.

Unfortunately for Perrin, in 1555 some of his more hotheaded followers started an anti-French protest that rapidly degenerated into a riot, with people running through the streets yelling "Kill the French!" Rioting was viewed in the sixteenth century as equivalent to sedition, and the crackdown by the government was swift and severe. Perrin fled the city into exile along with many of his followers; others were caught and tried, and some were executed. In the midst of all of this, Calvin stayed on the sidelines. He was not involved in the trials or in any of the backlash against Perrin, but then again, he didn't need to be. The effect of this incident was to strengthen Calvin's effective control of the city by eliminating all of the significant opposition to him and to his program. And it opened Geneva up to an even greater flood of refugees from France.

We should note, however, that Calvin's influence was never a matter of sheer political power. Calvin never staged a coup, and he never controlled the wheels of government. In principle, as a pastor, Calvin was simply a civil servant who could be fired on twenty-four hours' notice. He never even became a full citizen of the city; he spent most of his time there simply as a resident, and only toward the end of his life did he become a *bourgeois,* a lower-level citizen. Calvin's influence was based primarily on his massive intellect and moral authority rather than on political power or control as we would normally define it.

Calvin would spend the rest of his life in Geneva. During his time in the city, he contributed tremendously to the development of Protestantism, both organizationally and theologically. We turn next to his ideas of church structure and to two of the theological controversies in which he was involved.

Questions for Discussion

1. As we have seen, Calvin taught himself theology, yet he became arguably the most important theologian of the Protestant Reformation. Can you think of any parallel examples in the church or in any other areas? Do you think this would be possible in any field (including in the church) today? Why or why not?

2. What do you think of the stories of Calvin's and Luther's marriages? Why do you think they succeeded, when over half of marriages in America end in divorce?

3. Even though Calvin (like all the major reformers) believed in a state church, to what extent can we trace

our ideas of the separation of church and state to him? In Calvin's system, church and state cooperate in areas of mutual interest, but otherwise each is sovereign in its own sphere. How does this compare to the US Constitution?

4. Compare the refugee problem in Geneva with immigration politics in the United States. How does the French problem in Geneva compare to the political clout of refugee communities in the United States (e.g. Cubans in Florida)?

CHAPTER NINE

"The Most Perfect School of Christ"

Although Calvin is best known today for his theological ideas, notably predestination, arguably his biggest contribution to Christianity was his development of a distinctively Protestant church structure. He wasn't the first to do this, of course—he built on work done by Martin Bucer and many others—but Calvin's was unusually thorough and would influence a host of churches throughout the Protestant world. We thus need to spend some time with this topic here, and then move on to some of the more prominent theological controversies in his career.

Church Government

Before we get to Calvin's ideas of church structure, we should first ask whether church institutions are such a good idea in the first place. Hasn't the institutional church been the biggest obstacle facing the spread of the gospel? Don't the problems in the church hurt the reputation of Christianity in general? Wouldn't we be better off just preaching the gospel and not worrying about the institutional church? The answer is no. Aside from biblical arguments on the importance of the church, any social, cultural, or intellectual movement that is going to have an impact on society *must* institutionalize, or it will consign itself to futility. Institutionalization is a necessary part of the life cycle of any movement, even the most radical. Institutions serve to preserve and consolidate the insights of the first generation of leaders and to establish a base to develop and spread those ideas further. Without setting up church structures, writing confessions of faith, and so forth, the Reformation would have been doomed within a generation.

On to Calvin's church structure. Calvin argued that there were four offices in the church: pastors, doctors, elders, and deacons. Pastors were responsible for preaching and administering the sacraments, the two "marks" without which a true church does not exist. Doctors were teachers. Calvin originally saw these as professional theologians who could be consulted when questions arose in the church, though rather quickly the office was reduced to people teaching school on just about any level. It was possible to be both a doctor and a pastor—Calvin and his successor, Theodore Beza, were both—but they really are two separate offices. On the other hand, all pastors were also elders, along with a group of lay leaders. Elders were responsible for maintaining Christian moral standards in the community through a system of church discipline. (More on that in a minute.) Deacons were responsible for dealing with social welfare in the community, that is, taking care of widows, orphans, and those too old or too infirm to work. Calvin argued that there were two types of deacons: essentially fund-raisers and ecclesiastical social workers.

Along with these offices, Calvin also set up a number of organizations within the church through which these officers did their work. The Venerable Company of Pastors was a combination of a support group for the pastors and a theological advisory committee for the government. They weighed in on any subject about which they thought the government needed to hear their opinion. For the doctors, teaching centered primarily on pastoral preparation. In 1559, the Academy of Geneva was founded to train ministers both for service in Geneva and as missionaries to other parts of Europe. The Academy and its less formal predecessors are arguably among the most important but least studied institutions in Geneva. To gauge its impact consider the following: The Lutheran Reformation spread through about half the Holy Roman Empire and part of Scandinavia, with a short-term impact in England and German areas in eastern Europe. Calvinism spread from Switzerland to France, the Netherlands, parts of Germany, Bohemia, Hungary, Poland, England, Scotland, and the New World, and had followers for a time in Italy. Part of the reason for this was the welcome Geneva gave to religious refugees, as discussed in the last chapter. But even more than that, some of these refugees got the opportunity to receive high quality theological training, and then returned to their home countries as missionary pastors. They would then found Calvinist churches and would have an enormous impact on the religious life of their countries.

The combination of openness to refugees and the high-end training available in Geneva made the city a major center for international Protestantism, a result no one could have predicted when the city kicked out its bishop in 1536. But Calvin's influence and the institutions he established put the city on the map as a theological powerhouse. The doctors and pastors also held adult Bible studies, known as congregations. We will see an example of one of these later in the chapter.

The institution run by the deacons was the General Hospital. The Hospital was a comprehensive social welfare agency that handled everything but communicable diseases. It grew out of an attempt to organize the social welfare work of the city. Under the bishop, there had been a bewildering variety of church organizations involved in social welfare, each with its own ideas and target population. When the city drove out the Catholic clergy, the government took over the job of providing relief for the poor in the city. The Hospital took in orphans and taught them a trade, often grinding grain or baking bread with wheat from farms owned by the Hospital itself. The bread was then distributed to the deserving poor and those out of work due to illness or injury. It was thus a rationalized, centralized system similar to organizations established in other cities in the period. Calvin essentially baptized an existing institution, naming its officers deacons and saying that the Hospital was doing precisely what biblical deacons were intended to do.

The Hospital only helped native Genevans. The large refugee communities in the city had needy members too, and so the wealthier members of these communities established charitable funds to help their own poor. The officers of these funds were also generally recognized as deacons as well.

And then there's the consistory.

The Consistory

Of all the institutions in Calvin's Geneva, none is as well known and as poorly understood as the consistory. The consistory was charged with enforcing morality, and because of its work, Calvin's Geneva has been portrayed as a theocratic police state. One historian even described the consistory as instituting a "moral reign of terror" in the city. This impression comes largely because the minutes of the meetings were written in a form of sixteenth-century Genevan briefhand by a scribe with genuinely appalling handwriting that few people can actually read. Some excerpts were published in the nineteenth century that focused on all the really juicy cases, and most studies of the consistory until very recently were based entirely on those excerpts. Recently, however, the consistory registers have begun to be published, and studies of them show that the previously published excerpts distort the normal work of the consistory.

In terms of makeup, the consistory included the city's pastors, plus representatives from the civil government drawn from each district of the city. The presiding officer was the first syndic, one of the main officials in the city government. The consistory thus was a mixed court, including personnel from both church and state, with a civil official as moderator. In addition, the consistory had a scribe and an "officer," whose job it was to summon people to whom the consistory wished to speak.

In its early years, the consistory's primary concern was religious practices. Those called before the consistory for anything were questioned on their religious practices. The dialogue generally went something like this:

"Do you pray?"
"Yes, of course."

143

"What do you say?"

"*Pater noster, qui es in coeli . . .*"

"Wait a minute. That's Latin. You're a cobbler. Do you know Latin?"

"No."

"Then why do you pray like that?"

"That's how the priest taught it to me."

"OK, you need to learn the Lord's Prayer in a language you know. Do you say any other prayers?"

"Yes. *Ave Maria . . .*"

"Hold it. . . ."

People were also asked if they knew the Apostles' Creed and the Ten Commandments; if they did not, they were sent to church to learn them. The consistory would also check for other questionable religious practices, as well as magic, charms, superstition, and so forth. These became less and less common over time as a result of the city's sustained campaign to "Protestantize" the populace.

After religious questions, the next most common problem involved interpersonal conflict: public quarreling, excessive beating of wives by husbands (and occasionally husbands by wives), excessive nagging of husbands by wives (and occasionally wives by husbands), being drunk and disorderly, and so forth. The elders usually cleared these types of problems up without recourse to the consistory. Only if the people involved failed to agree to mediation did it go to the consistory itself.

The next most common offense was various types of sexual irregularities, such as fornication, adultery, bestiality, and homosexuality. This category also included breach of marriage promises. In this period, a verbal agreement to marry was tantamount to a marriage; it was legally binding. When someone tried to dissolve the promise or deny it had been made, the case could come before the consistory. This was a fairly common occurrence, and accounts for a significant number of the cases in this category. It is worth noting that the consistory was not overly focused on sexual offenses, nor did it pry into people's bedrooms. Its primary concern was on public morality, that is, on situations that became public knowledge and thus could cause a scandal. It did police private behavior, to be sure, in order to create a godly society. But this was a goal of all governments in this period, and in most cases, the churches played a role in this. Geneva's system was in many ways no more intrusive than many others.

The next most common type of case was anything else.

In terms of sanctions, most often someone who was brought before the consistory got a good tongue lashing. Although it is not always clear from the consistory registers who delivered these, Calvin seems to have done it pretty often; he had a sharp temper and was trained in rhetoric.

Alternately, and perhaps as a stiffer sanction, one could be told to attend more sermons. If one's offense was particularly serious, one might be told to confess one's sins publicly after the main church service. This kind of public shaming was quite common and very effective, given that maintaining one's honor was extremely important in this period. If the offense was also a crime, the person could be sent to the civil government for further action.

Beyond these, the consistory had only one other sanction at its disposal: excommunication. This was reserved only for those who refused to acknowledge their fault before the consistory. Excommunicants were prohibited from participating in the sacraments, whether baptism or Communion. Given the important social role these two sacraments played in Genevan life, this was a pretty stiff penalty, and most people reconciled with the consistory either before the next Lord's Supper or immediately thereafter.

So how well did the consistory do in reforming public life? Visitors to Geneva frequently commented on the safety of the city and on the high moral standards of the community. John Knox commented in a letter that Geneva was "the most perfect school of Christ" on earth, and noted that the pure gospel was preached in many places, but only in Geneva was it actually lived. And since the consistory was largely responsible for the moral quality of life in the city, wherever Calvinism went, consistory-like institutions almost inevitably followed. This was in keeping with the Calvinist emphasis on living an austere, godly life and the strong concern about personal piety and morality that became hallmarks of the Calvinist reformation.

And that is about it for the church government. Since Geneva was a city-state, there was no need for Calvin to develop church structures for larger geographic territories.

These would evolve on their own elsewhere, and we will look at them when we get to them. For now, one more point needs to be made before we move on.

Church-State Relations

Calvin's Geneva has often been described as a theocracy, with Calvin acting as the ayatollah of the Alps, a clerical dictator who enforced a strict, moralistic religion on a helpless society. This was far from the truth. Calvin insisted that church and state each has its own God-given functions, and neither should interfere with the workings of the other. On the other hand, no one in the sixteenth century believed that church and state could or should be completely separate. Religion and politics were inseparable in most people's minds, and few saw any reason to separate them completely. Calvin and many other reformers, however, did see them as operating in overlapping spheres. The state should not interfere in church affairs, including excommunication, arranging the preaching schedule, the sacraments, and other church functions. The church should not interfere with the civil government, though the pastors could and did give advice on religious questions, including foreign affairs. In an era in which religious wars gripped much of Europe, diplomacy inevitably connected to religion, but foreign affairs were still viewed as properly within the jurisdiction of the civil government. Other areas were not so simple. Protestants saw marriage as a civil function, yet its role in regulating sexual behavior also made it a moral question; the church, therefore, had a legitimate interest in questions relating to marriage. Similarly, the civil government had a stake in encouraging morality within the city and in promoting "true religion," but this was primarily a church responsibility. Because of these sorts of considerations, the consistory as a church institution included not only pastors but also representatives of the civil government, who became church elders. Social welfare was a civil matter, yet it again had moral overtones. So the men and women who ran the Hospital were employees of the civil government, but also deacons in the church.

The role of elders and deacons as employees of the civil government who are then made church officers has its parallel with the pastors and doctors; though officers in the church, they were also civil servants, drawing their salary from the state and subject to dismissal on twenty-four-hour notice. Unlike the elders, who had other professions and who served in the government and the church as a sideline, the pastors, doctors, and some of the deacons were full-time employees of the state. To put it differently, in Geneva, the church was staffed and paid for by the state, not the other way around. This was the practice in virtually all parts of Protestant Europe.

The real irony is that it is precisely the relative independence of the church from the state—its freedom to act in its own legitimate sphere without state interference—that has contributed to the idea that Geneva was a theocracy. The independence went both ways; the state was not to interfere with those areas that were the church's concern, and the church couldn't interfere with the state in its work. They therefore had to work together in areas where their legitimate interests overlapped, such as enforcement of morality and taking care of the poor. But through it all, the church remained a branch of the civil government.

Another reason behind Calvin's reputation for running a theocracy comes from some well publicized heresy trials that took place in Geneva on his watch. There were heresy trials in other parts of Europe, but these have stuck to Calvin far more than similar trials elsewhere. We turn now to these trials and to Calvin and theological controversy. We begin with Jerome Bolsec, who first brought predestination front and center in discussions of Calvin's theology, and then turn to the Servetus affair.

Predestination

To understand this controversy, we need to define predestination and see why it is important. The idea behind predestination is that our salvation depends on God and not on ourselves. Although there are a number of passages in Scripture that talk about it (e.g. Rom. 8:29–30 or Eph. 1), it didn't become a major subject in theology until the fourth century. A British monk named Pelagius had argued that our salvation depended entirely on the choices we make; both original sin and substitutionary atonement are false, according to Pelagius, since neither Adam's guilt, nor ours, nor the merits of Christ can be imputed to another person. You are on your own before God. Some people in the church were heavily influenced by Pelagius, but others rejected his ideas. The most important of the latter was Augustine of Hippo. Augustine thought Pelagius's ideas were not only false but downright dangerous. Christ is the author of our salvation—it depends on what he has done, not what we have done. As a result, the decision about salvation is in God's hands, not ours. And this is a good thing, since none of us deserves to be saved on the basis of our own merits. We have all sinned, and as a result, no one deserves blessings from God; salvation is a result of us getting what we *don't* deserve, not what we do.

At this point, we need to distinguish between two different

versions of the doctrine of predestination. *Single predestination* argues that God chooses some people for salvation and judges others according to their own merits. Of course, that means they'll be damned, since no one measures up to God's infinite standard of holiness. *Double predestination,* on the other hand, argues that God has a plan for everyone's life—for some, it is heaven, for others, it is hell. God chooses everyone to either fly or fry; he doesn't just leave us to our fate. This is a more severe version of the doctrine than single predestination, though there's no practical difference between the two in terms of the fate of those not chosen for salvation. There is some dispute about Augustine's views. Most scholars argue that he held to single predestination, while others are equally sure he held to double predestination.

Whatever Augustine's views, he won, and Pelagianism was declared a heresy. Between Augustine's day and the sixteenth century, many variations of the doctrine of salvation emerged, with differing degrees of emphasis on human contributions to salvation. Pelagianism was out, but then there's semi-Pelagianism, semi-Augustinianism, Augustinianism, hyper-Augustinianism, and so forth. Catholic theology generally fell somewhere between Pelagianism and Augustinianism.

Luther, as an Augustinian monk, obviously was familiar with the history of the debate. After his Tower Experience, he adamantly rejected any hint of Pelagianism: We are saved by grace—God's undeserved favor—and grace alone, and that comes from faith and faith alone. But faith itself is a gift of God; it doesn't come from our actions or decisions. But this means that God makes the decisions. If our salvation depended on our decision or on our responding to God in faith, then that decision or response would become the work that saves us, an idea Luther adamantly rejected. As a result, Luther recognized the need for predestination. It is a logical consequence of *sola gratia* and *sola fide,* and besides, it is a good scriptural term. But Luther was not willing to go any further than that. He believed that Scripture taught predestination, but he did not think it told us how it worked. So he simply said it happened and left it at that.

Calvin, on the other hand, thought that Scripture taught double predestination. At the same time, he did not think that it was an issue most people needed to deal with. Calvin was more interested in preaching the fundamentals of the faith and applying Scripture to life than in teaching about predestination, particularly because the discussion would likely distract from more important issues. So Calvin taught predestination in his theological works and biblical commentaries, but not from the pulpit. He simply did not want to focus on it in his public ministry. Unfortunately, he was not given the chance to leave it in the background.

The Bolsec Controversy

Jerome Bolsec was a former monk and Catholic theologian who had converted to Protestantism and moved to Geneva. He was working as the personal physician of one of the nobles who lived outside the city and had become familiar with Calvin and his writings. He didn't like Calvin personally and was irked by his ideas on predestination. So Bolsec took it upon himself to cause problems for Calvin with predestination as a wedge issue. His plan was simple. Calvin had too many things to do to attend the congregations (adult Bible studies), so Bolsec decided to go to one of them, and when the pastor asked if there were any questions, he would launch into his attack, whether or not the passage being studied had any connection to predestination at all. Word would spread from there, and Calvin would never be able to get the lid on it; he'd be discredited, and Geneva would get rid of him. It was an ingenious plan, except for one slight miscalculation. Calvin was free that evening and showed up at the congregation. When Bolsec finished his presentation—remember, he had come gunning for bear—all eyes turned to Calvin to see how he would respond. Keep in mind that Calvin had no formal theological training and that he was caught flat-footed by Bolsec. Despite this, he launched into a well reasoned, well argued, and well presented case, citing from memory extensive passages of Scripture and the church fathers verbatim. His presentation was so convincing that when it was over, one of the magistrates promptly arrested Bolsec for heresy.

Calvin was furious with Bolsec, not simply because he disagreed with Calvin on predestination, but because of the underhanded way he went about his attack. As a result, Calvin was out for blood at the trial. Bolsec was in fact convicted, but the Small Council overruled Calvin and argued that Bolsec's heresy wasn't sufficiently grave to warrant his execution. He was banished, though, and made his way to France. After starting a number of controversies in the Reformed churches there, he converted back to Catholicism and wrote a libelous (and fictitious) biography of Calvin that became a staple of anti-Calvin propaganda.

Bolsec did succeed in one part of his program, however: He made Calvin's views on predestination a very public issue. Lutherans, who never really trusted Calvin because of his views on the Lord's Supper, quickly picked up on it and began attacking Calvin as a heretic. Ironically, these attacks soon led the Lutherans themselves to abandon predestination altogether, forgetting the fact that Luther himself accepted it. Calvin couldn't let these challenges go unanswered, of course, and thus he ended up spending a considerable amount of energy defending his views on a doctrine he didn't particularly want to focus on in his public ministry.

Servetus and Anti-Trinitarianism

Calvin also had a famous run-in with Servetus, an anti-Trinitarian radical reformer. Anti-Trinitarians were people who rejected some aspect of the traditional formulation of the doctrine of the Trinity. They tended to be highly educated—they were, after all, raising an intellectual question about the faith—and to come from areas on the borders of Europe near Muslim territories, such as Spain, Hungary, or Transylvania. Servetus was a Spanish physician who had studied at the same college at the University of Paris and at the same time with Calvin; it is likely that the two knew each other. Also like Calvin, Servetus was a self-trained theologian, though the two came to completely different conclusions on doctrine. Servetus decided that the doctrine of the Trinity was inaccurate as usually formulated. He believed that in order for the incarnation to have any real meaning, the second person in the Trinity needed to come into existence at that time. Thus, prior to the incarnation, God existed as just the Father and the Spirit; after the incarnation, the Godhead acquired an extra person and now exists as a Trinity. He wrote up his ideas in a treatise called "On the Errors of the Trinity," a title calculated to attract attention. It did, and Servetus was forced to go into hiding to avoid being tried for heresy.

While living under an assumed name in southern France, Servetus continued to work on theological questions, combining them with medical research. For example, Servetus dissected human cadavers in the hope of finding the location of the soul. In the process, he discovered the pulmonary circulation of blood decades before Sir William Harvey, who is usually credited with the discovery. Servetus wrote all of this up, combined it with work on medicinal syrups and some bizarre theological speculations, and published it in a book called *On the Restitution of Christianity*. He then sent a copy to Calvin with a pseudonymous letter asking for his reaction. Calvin saw through the ruse, but decided to play along anyway. He wrote to Servetus using the pseudonym from the original letter, telling him that the work was heretical and admonishing him to have nothing to do with it.

Meanwhile, a Catholic layman sent a letter to Geneva, calling on its citizens to return to Catholicism and asking them why they tolerated such a notorious heretic as Calvin. Calvin replied, saying that the Catholics tolerated much more serious heretics, such as Servetus, in their territories, so they should not pester Geneva about Calvin. This caught the attention of the Catholic authorities, and they asked him if he really knew where Servetus was. Calvin replied that he did, and that they would find him in a particular town in France. The inquisition promptly arrested Servetus, tried him for heresy, and sentenced him to death. Before the sentence could be carried out, Servetus escaped from prison. He then made his way to Geneva; once there, he decided to attend church on Sunday, found out where Calvin was preaching, and sat in the front row. You have to wonder if the guy had a death wish, though I suspect he probably thought he could convince Calvin he was right. In this, Servetus would prove seriously mistaken. Calvin spotted him, and as soon as the service was over Servetus was arrested.

To make a long story short, Servetus was convicted of heresy. Calvin and Beza testified for the prosecution as expert theologians. The transcripts of the trial were sent around to get input from Zurich, Bern, Basel, and Schaffhausen; since the Catholics had already sentenced him to death, these were about the only groups Geneva could ask. The verdict came back unanimously: He is a major heretic; kill him. Calvin was good with this, so he advocated beheading him in order to get this out of the way quickly and quietly; the trial had already given Servetus far too much attention. But the Small Council disagreed—you beheaded noblemen; you burned heretics. Calvin objected vehemently, but to no avail, and Servetus was sentenced to be burned alive. Calvin refused to participate in the execution, so Beza stepped in as a representative for the pastors. His job was to urge Servetus to repent, and to report it if he did. He did not. Servetus's last words were "Jesus, son of the eternal God, have mercy on me." Beza commented later that if Servetus had only said, "Jesus, eternal son of God, have mercy on me," the whole thing would have been unnecessary. So Servetus was executed for a misplaced adjective.

The burning of Servetus is a blemish on Calvin's career,

but it does need to be put in context. Calvin did lead the inquisition to Servetus; when Servetus came to church, Calvin did have him arrested; he did testify at the trial. His desire to behead rather than burn Servetus is hardly a mitigating factor. On the other hand, the unanimous consent of the Catholic and Protestant churches to Servetus's death does need to be taken into account. In this era, heresy was considered more serious than murder; a murderer only kills your body; the heretic threatens your soul. Further, any society that tolerated heretics was inviting divine judgment. Thus, the death penalty was considered perfectly appropriate for heresy, both because of the seriousness of the crime and because of the need to cleanse the society from the pollution the heretic brought with him. The plaque to Servetus in Geneva describes him as the victim of an intolerant age; that is as good an epitaph as any for the event.

This did not exactly end the Servetus affair, however. Some time earlier, a man by the name of Castellio had been a teacher in Geneva. He wanted to become a pastor, but due to a disagreement over how to interpret the Song of Solomon, Calvin opposed his ordination. Castellio, disappointed, left Geneva for Basel, carrying with him a very positive attestation from Calvin about Castellio's abilities as a teacher. When he heard about the Servetus affair, Castellio was furious. Servetus wasn't a dangerous heretic like Thomas Munzer or the Anabaptists at Münster, or even the Swiss Brethren, whose rebaptism of adults threatened the social fabric in the community. Rather, he was prosecuted simply for what he thought, for his ideas. Castellio wrote a book entitled *On the Coercion of Heretics,* in which he argued that prosecuting heretics was counterproductive: Servetus's ideas would have sunk like rocks if Calvin hadn't made a capital case out of them. In fact, because of what Calvin did, Servetus's ideas were much better known than they would have been otherwise. If the person commits no physical crime, he should not be subject to prosecution, and thus heretics ought to be tolerated in society. Calvin and Beza were outraged at the book and appealed to the authorities in Basel to do something about Castellio. They didn't, and Castellio would end up writing other books against religious warfare and promoting peace, harmony, and other outlandish ideas. But he was largely a voice in the wilderness; very few other people in Europe were ready for arguments for toleration.

Despite these controversies, Calvin's ideas spread widely and helped shape religious thinking in a number of areas in Europe. We turn to some of these in the next three chapters.

Questions for Discussion

1. How do you view the role of institutionalization in the church? Is it a good or bad thing? Why?
2. With the number of church choices available today, is church discipline possible in our society? Do you think we need it? Why or why not? If so, under what circumstances should we exercise it, and how should it be done? Do you know any churches that have an active disciplinary system in place? If so, how does it work? Is it effective?
3. What do you think of free will and predestination? How do you defend your views? Have you looked into the arguments for the other side?
4. Are there ever any grounds for punishing someone for what he or she thinks? Is this different from hate crimes legislation, which prescribes additional penalties on the basis of the perpetrator's motivation for an act (i.e., what he or she was thinking) on top of the penalties for the act itself? Why or why not?

CHAPTER TEN

Spain and the Dutch Revolt

With Charles V's abdication, Philip II of Spain inherited all of Charles V's dynastic possessions except the family's original territories in Austria, but he lost the title of emperor. Even without the empire, however, Philip inherited a significant chunk of the earth's surface. He owned Spain through his grandmother Joan the Mad, and with Spain Sicily, southern Italy, Milan, Mediterranean islands such as the Balearics and Sardinia, and the Spanish possessions in the New World and Asia; from Philip "the Handsome" Habsburg, husband of Joan, he inherited the Low Countries and the Franche Comté, which Philip the Handsome had obtained from his mother, Mary of Burgundy. Then in 1580, the Portuguese royal line died out, and Philip II annexed Portugal and all of its colonies in the New World, Africa, and Asia. Spain was the most powerful state in the world and the biggest and first truly global empire in history.

Curiously, despite this enormous empire and the influx of gold and silver from the New World, Philip's finances were never particularly stable. Spain was a rural country whose principle export was the wool of Merino sheep, the highest quality of raw wool available at the time, but hardly a major moneymaker in the grand scheme of things. Further, of all the countries of Europe, Spain was probably the least prepared for the challenges of colonization; it had little skilled industry or manufacturing to provide the finished goods the colonists wanted in return for their gold and silver. As a result, the hard currency that flowed into Spain flowed right out again to purchase manufactured goods for the colonies, mostly to northern Italy and the Low Countries. To make matters worse, Spain was constantly involved in wars outside its borders. Philip was a devout, conservative Catholic who saw it as his duty to defend and promote the faith against both Muslim expansion and Protestant heretics. So he spent the majority of his reign fighting wars, mostly though not entirely over religion. Although he never got the opportunity to launch a crusade, Philip's naval forces played a key role in halting Ottoman expansion in the eastern Mediterranean at the battle of Lepanto (1571). He intervened in the French Wars of Religion on the ultra-Catholic side, and also found himself in a nonreligious war in southern Italy. But the most important war of his reign was a revolt against his rule in the Netherlands that would also lead to conflict with England.

The Origins of the Dutch Revolt

The Low Countries (a.k.a. the Netherlands or, today, the Benelux countries—*Be*lgium-*Ne*therlands-*Lux*embourg) had become a Habsburg possession with the marriage of Maximilian I Habsburg to Mary of Burgundy. Charles V, their grandson, actually grew up in Ghent and considered the region his homeland. As a result, even though the Netherlands ignored many of his edicts—particularly those that made Protestantism not only a religious but a civil offense—they stayed pretty loyal to him and were a critical part of his empire; fully half of Charles's crown revenues came from the Low Countries. Philip, on the other hand, grew up in Spain and didn't even speak the local language; in fact, he was considered a foreign king by many in the Netherlands. Worse, he did not understand (and did not want to understand) the fundamental ethos of the area. The Low Countries were one of only two heavily urbanized areas in Europe, with over half the population living in towns and cities. Like most medieval cities, these were typically republics, run by representative councils drawn from the better-off segments of society, and they guarded their privileges jealously. Religious views in the Netherlands tended toward a low-key Erasmian style of reform. Catholics, Lutherans, Anabaptists, and Reformed Protestants all tended to get along reasonably well, and a tone of moderation generally prevailed. The late 1550s saw a growing militancy among the Protestants, however, as more and more Calvinist refugees from France and missionary pastors from Geneva entered the Low Countries and began to win converts across the social spectrum. By 1561 they were numerous enough to hold a synod, adopt a Calvinist statement of faith known as the Belgic Confession (based on the 1559 French Gallican Confession), and set up a church order paralleling that of the Huguenots.

Philip's greatest asset in the Low Countries was his half-sister, Margaret of Parma. Charles V's illegitimate daughter, Margaret was raised in Ghent and was thus considered a Fleming by the locals, despite having been married to the nephews of two popes and having spent a considerable amount of time in Italy. Her excellent equestrian abilities earned her additional respect from the nobility. Had Margaret been allowed to govern the Low Countries, she might have kept things on a relatively even keel, but Philip was a control freak; he insisted that Margaret carry out policies established in Madrid. He demanded, for example, that she carry out Charles's edicts against the Protestants, and he introduced the inquisition into the Low Countries in 1559; he also forced her to accept Antoine Perronet de Granvelle (1517–1586), bishop of Arras, archbishop of Malines (after 1561), and his favorite at court, as her principal advisor. Granvelle was pushing a policy of centralization on the Low Countries, a territory united only by a common desire to remain disunited. It has been said that if you have one Dutch man you have a theologian; two, you have a church; and three, you have a split. For their part, the leaders of the Netherlands saw their king in very medieval terms as a first among equals, and were not about to give up their autonomy. They also resented the presence of Spanish troops in their lands and the taxes Philip imposed to pay for them.

The Protestants, feeling the pressure, appealed to the town councils for help. Their argument was that Philip was illegally usurping the towns' rights and autonomy under the law. The town councils agreed and protested to Margaret. Two members of her council, Lamoraal, count of Egmont and prince of Gavre, and William of Nassau, prince of Orange (known as William the Silent because of his diplomatic skills and discretion), led the opposition to Philip's policies. Their protests led Philip to withdraw his troops in 1560. But Philip reorganized the bishoprics in his territories, making Granvelle the de facto primate over the Low

Countries. Following Philip's directives, Granvelle revved the inquisition into high gear, though whenever possible the stadtholders declined to cooperate. William the Silent and Egmont formed a league with Philip of Montmorency, count of Hoorn, admiral of Flanders, and stadtholder of Gelderland and Zutphen, to oppose Granvelle. They got the support of other nobles, and in 1563 persuaded Philip to pull Granvelle from the Netherlands.

This didn't end the problem, however. Philip, in the name of church reform, now insisted that Margaret enforce both the decrees of the Council of Trent and the laws against heresy, and that the Jesuits be admitted into the territory. The council of state protested that the Tridentine decrees undermined the traditional privileges of the states, and demanded that they be modified and the persecutions eased. Hundreds of nobles and other community leaders met in secret and signed a document called the Compromise, in which they pledged to protect the persecuted and oppose the inquisition while outwardly remaining loyal to the king. In 1566, a group of about 250 excitable young men presented a petition to Margaret demanding an end to the inquisition, a softening of the decrees against heresy, a moratorium on enforcing the Tridentine decrees, and the calling of the Estates General. Margaret's advisors told her to ignore "these beggars"; soon, the opponents of the king proudly adopted the name of Beggars for their movement. Margaret, for her part, referred their petition to Philip. This didn't sit well with the "Beggars," however, and a visible and vocal movement against the king began growing.

Iconoclasm and Occupation

At about this point, there was a fairly widespread outbreak of iconoclasm in the Low Countries, and images in churches, stained glass windows, and statues were smashed. This event is widely misunderstood. First, it was aimed specifically at property, not people. In one case, when an individual accidentally toppled a statue that damaged a tomb, he was executed for desecrating a grave, the trial being conducted by the very people involved in the iconoclasm. Second, the outbreak is usually blamed on radical Calvinist preachers, but they actually preached against it. Calvinists may have been radical in some ways, but they were adamantly opposed to any kind of social unrest. Recent research actually suggests that the iconoclasm was a result of *Philip's* policies, not the Calvinists'. When Philip talked about supporting church reform, what he meant was stamping out Protestantism, restructuring the church, and enforcing Trent. What church reform meant to the people of the Netherlands was Protestant reforms, in many cases including the removal of images à la Zwingli; hence the iconoclasm. The stadtholders seemed unable to stop the unrest. Louis of Nassau decided to look for military assistance from French and German Protestants, while William the Silent left the country for Germany. Margaret was largely left to deal with the situation herself. She managed to restore order relatively quickly, at least in terms of the iconoclasm, but she still had the "Beggars," plus public worship by Calvinist congregations, to deal with.

When Philip heard about the iconoclasm, he decided he needed to break the back of the heretics once and for all. Pope Pius V counseled moderation: Offer amnesty to the upper classes and only go after the real leaders. Philip, though, would have none of that. Instead, he sent in 10,000 veteran soldiers under Fernando Alvarez de Toledo, duke of Alva, the ruthless, brutal general who had won the battle of Muhlberg for Charles V. It took them four months to march from Genoa to the Low Countries

along the "Spanish Road" across the Alps, through the Franche-Comté, Lorraine, and Luxembourg, arriving in Brussels in August 1567. Alva was given complete military and political authority in the Netherlands, and through a combination of treachery and military efficiency, he got effective control over the Low Countries in short order. He established a new tribunal known as the "Council of Blood," which tried "heretics and traitors" (the same thing in Alva's eyes). Between 6,000 and 8,000 people were tried, convicted, and executed in 1568, including Egmont and Montmorency, despite the traditional rights, privileges, and protections of the nobility. Margaret, disillusioned and disgusted by Alva, resigned her regency and returned to Parma.

Nationalism, Religion, and the Disunited Provinces

As if the Council of Blood had not done enough damage, Alva went on to alienate everyone he had not gotten to yet. In 1569 he forced the Estates General to adopt a sales tax based on Spanish precedents. This may have worked in rural Spain, but in a territory run by manufacturing and commerce, it virtually paralyzed the entire economy and drove the merchants and guild members into an alliance with the nobles and Calvinists who had been leading the revolt. William the Silent took advantage of this situation and of Admiral Coligny's lobbying of Charles IX of France for help for the revolt. William returned to the northern provinces and began attacking Spanish forces in 1571 with the help of Huguenots and German Protestant mercenaries. Although not a man of strong religious convictions— he had changed faiths three times by 1560—he realized that it would take a militant brand of Protestantism to defeat Philip's militant Catholicism. So William decided to court the Calvinists, with the result that nationalism and Calvinism merged in the Netherlands. Meanwhile, Dutch privateers known as the "Sea Beggars" began raiding Spanish shipping and even defeated a Spanish fleet in the Zuider Zee. The Sea Beggars initially operated out of English ports, but Elizabeth eventually turned her back on them, so they seized the cities of Brill and Flushing, and from there established control of the maze of islands and waterways along the northern and central coasts of the Low Countries. The Sea Beggars' success provided some protection against Spanish attack in the north.

After the St. Bartholomew's Day Massacres in 1572, however, Alva no longer needed to fear an attack from France. Accordingly, he turned all his attention on the northern provinces that had been leading the fight up to that time. Unfortunately, however, the Dutch did not play fair; they would not meet him in open battle, and opened dikes to flood the lands the Spanish army occupied or were trying to cross. Alva realized he would not be able to make much headway, and in 1573 asked to be relieved of his command. In his place, Philip appointed Don Luis de Requesens, with instructions to get rid of the sales tax and to offer an amnesty for all but heretics, on condition that they put down their arms and submit unconditionally to Philip's authority. This proposal was not exactly greeted with enthusiasm, so the war continued. The one really notable event was the failure of the Spanish siege of Leiden in 1574. In honor of this victory, the Dutch founded the University of Leiden, the first Protestant university in the Netherlands, a year after the siege was lifted.

Requesens died of typhus in 1576 and was succeeded by Don Juan, Philip's half-brother and the commander of the victorious Catholic forces at Lepanto. His governorship didn't start off on the right foot; unpaid Spanish and Italian troops decided to sack the city of Antwerp at a time when it was loyal to Spain and under Spanish control. The "Spanish Fury," as the sack was called, destroyed what little credibility Philip had left. Representatives of thirteen of the provinces met in Ghent under the leadership of William the Silent to set terms for a cessation of hostilities. All Spanish troops were to be withdrawn, all edicts against heresy were to be lifted, the religious issues were to be decided by the Estates General, but Spain was to remain at least a nominal overlord of the Low Countries. William was made the supreme commander of the forces of the United Provinces while the war continued. These conditions were set down in a treaty known as the Pacification of Ghent (1576). When Don Juan arrived the following June with orders to negotiate, he met with the Estates General with the Pacification as the basis for the discussion. Don Juan was forced to sign the Perpetual Edict, which guaranteed the traditional rights and privileges of the provinces and promised to release political prisoners and withdraw Spanish troops on condition that the provinces give them their back pay and that Catholicism remain in place. Holland and Zeeland refused to go along with this and walked out of the Estates General. Don Juan grew tired of negotiating and in any event could not live up to his side of the bargain, so he withdrew and called on Philip to send more troops. The Estates General declared him an enemy of the state, and William was greeted as a hero even in Brussels. But his success was ephemeral. To the traditional ethnic, linguistic, and cultural rivalries between the provinces was added a new source of division: The southern provinces were largely Catholic, while the north was largely Calvinist. By 1578, cleavages were becoming obvious in William's coalition, just as 20,000 more veteran troops arrived under Alessandro Farnese, son of Margaret of Parma.

Courting France and England

Farnese was arguably the most effective general of the era, as well as an able diplomat. He routed the forces of the Low Countries and drove them north in January 1578; when Don Juan died in October, Farnese was appointed governor in his place. He entered negotiations with the majority Catholic cities and provinces in the south, getting them to accept Philip and Catholicism in the Union of Arras (1579). William responded by organizing the northern states into the Union of Utrecht. Philip's counter to this was to declare William an outlaw and put a price on his head. This had the effect of making William more popular with the people, and prompted William to renounce Spanish overlordship in his *Apology,* presented before the Estates General in December 1580. This was the first application of the political theory of the *Vindicae contra tyrannos* (1579), written by an anonymous Huguenot in response to the St. Bartholomew's Day Massacre, which

argued that the people had a moral duty to remove mon-
archs who had descended into tyranny. In an effort to gain
political support, William convinced Archduke Matthias
Habsburg of Austria (a future Holy Roman Emperor) to
become a stadtholder of the Netherlands—hoping thereby
to split Philip's branch of the family from the Austrian
Habsburgs—and negotiated with Francis, duke of Alençon
and Anjou, brother of Henri III of France, to become
"Defender of the Liberty of the Low Countries." Since
Anjou was a favored suitor of Queen Elizabeth, this
appointment was intended to bring in both France and
England on the side of the Netherlands. Anjou agreed to
supply money and men to the United Provinces in return
for his title, much to the annoyance of Henri III, in return
for recognition of his sovereignty over the Low Countries.
The northern Estates General agreed, except in Holland
and Zeeland where William retained his full sovereignty as
governor. In the Act of Abjuration (1581), the Estates
General declared Philip deposed and Francis his successor
as duke of Brabant.

Unfortunately, once Francis arrived in 1582, his character and manners alienated the people from him. The fact
that he was Catholic didn't help either. In the meantime,
a Portuguese merchant fallen on hard times had one of his
clerks try to assassinate William. Miraculously, the shot
went through his cheeks and jaw but did not kill him.
While he was recovering in Antwerp, Francis decided to
seize power and attempted to storm the city in the so-
called "French Fury." It did not work. Despite this,
William continued to support Anjou because he believed
that the revolt would fail without French support (which
Anjou had failed to provide in any event, but that is
another matter). Meanwhile, Farnese continued to take
city after city. William was driven into the northern

provinces, where in 1584 an assassin got into his home and killed him. Anjou had died one month to the day before, so William's seventeen-year-old son Maurice of Nassau was selected by the Estates General to be the military commander of the remaining provinces, an area that was culturally, ethnically, and religiously more homogenous than the Low Countries as a whole, and whose defenders were tenacious and motivated by religion to continue the resistance.

Foreign support was not forthcoming, however. Henri III of France withdrew his protection from the revolt, so the Dutch appealed to Elizabeth I of England for help in 1585. She was reluctant to challenge Spain overtly, however, and only agreed to send 6,000 men under Robert Dudley, earl of Leicester, in return for a substantial cash contribution to the crown. Dudley was appointed governor-general with almost unlimited authority, though without receiving Elizabeth's prior authorization for the post. He botched the situation badly, however, alienating Catholics with his radical Protestantism, alienating the merchants by interfering with trade, alienating the states by ignoring traditional privileges, and so on. (Incidentally, he had good reason for some of his actions: Spain had at best limited manufacturing capabilities, whereas the Dutch had largely replaced Italy as the principal manufacturing region of Europe. Spain bought many of the manufactured goods for its colonies and, even more bizarre, actually acquired much of its military equipment from the Dutch, while at the same time fighting them. So the Spanish were enriching the Dutch and the Dutch were arming their attackers. It was this trade that Dudley tried to stop. But from the Dutch perspective, business was business.) Dudley returned to England in 1587, leaving the situation in some ways worse than it had been when he arrived.

The Dutch on Their Own

Since neither France nor England could help, the Dutch were thrown back on their own resources. Fortunately, these were considerable. Maurice of Nassau, with the help of his cousin William Louis of Nassau, studied ancient Roman texts on military science and came up with a new system for using firearms that relied on extensive drilling, advancing, and retreating in rows, firing in volleys, and a host of other innovations that made the Dutch infantry one of the most effective in Europe. The Dutch were even more successful at sea, having the largest merchant marine in Europe, the best ships, and better guns than the Spanish. The Spanish, meanwhile, had their own problems. Philip's failed invasion of England with the Armada (1588) and his decision to intervene in the French Wars of Religion on the side of the Catholic League diverted Farnese's forces and kept him from concentrating his efforts on retaking the rebellious provinces. When Farnese died in 1592, he was succeeded by Archduke Ernest of Austria, who only put minimal efforts into the war. The net result was that Spanish forces were completely driven out of the northern provinces in 1593. When Ernest died, he was replaced by Archduke Albert, who did no better than Ernest had. Things became worse for the Spanish when Henri IV came to the French throne. Henri and Elizabeth made alliances with the United Provinces and recognized their independence in 1596. That same year, the long years of war and Dutch and English raiding of Spain's colonies and trading and treasure fleets took its toll, and Philip was forced to declare bankruptcy.

Although Spain made peace with France in 1598, the war with the Dutch continued. Philip II died that year and was succeeded by his weak and incompetent son, Philip III.

Genetics may have something to do with Philip's abilities: Philip II had married Anna of Austria, who was his first cousin through her mother and his first cousin once removed through her father. Philip III was thus seriously inbred. Albert of Austria, Spain's regent in the Netherlands, married Philip III's half-sister Isabella and received the southern provinces as a separate state, with the condition that they revert to Spain if Albert and Isabella died without heir. The Spanish made peace with England in 1604, but they made no headway in the northern provinces and continued to take serious losses at sea from Dutch privateers. Finally, in 1609, Spain needed a breather and agreed to the Twelve Years' Truce. This granted the United Provinces in the north virtual independence, pending the outcome of negotiations between Spain and the Dutch on a final settlement to the dispute. This was really a smokescreen; neither side was willing to budge, and both sides knew it. Spain needed the break to reorganize and gather its forces, and the Dutch were happy for the truce so they could continue their economic expansion. They were rapidly becoming a global economic superpower, and the Twelve Years' Truce gave them the time to cement their leading position in manufacturing, trade, and finance.

Tiptoeing to the TULIP

The Dutch Reformed Church also had to deal with a theological question with political overtones during the Twelve Years' Truce that would have long-term implications for international Calvinism. A Genevan-trained Dutch theologian named Arminius, supported by Johan van Oldenbarnevelt, an important figure in the government with Maurice of Nassau, challenged the official doctrine of the Dutch Reformed Church, arguing instead for a

liberal form of Calvinism that incorporated humanistic theology. After Arminius's death in 1609, his mantel was taken up by Johan Wtenbogaert, who presented the Remonstrance (or "protest") in 1610, challenging the Reformed Church's views on predestination. The party thus became known as the Remonstrants. Five points centered on ideas of free will stood out: Human beings were not so corrupted by original sin that they could not respond to God's grace on their own; they could choose to respond to God or to reject him freely; even as Christians, they were thus free to abandon him and lose their salvation; they were chosen by God on the basis of something within them, not by an arbitrary divine whim; and Christ's death paid for the sins of the whole world, not just of the elect. Oldenbarnevelt and the upper classes tended to support the Remonstrants.

The official church and the majority of the clergy and common people saw the Remonstrance as nothing short of heresy. Led by a theologian named Gomarus, they issued their Counter Remonstrance, which countered the five points of Arminianism with five points of their own. Maurice of Nassau eventually sided with the Counter Remonstrants, adding political and social dimensions to the theological quarrel, which pitted supporters of a decentralized political structure led by the patricians (Oldenbarnevelt, the upper classes, and the Remonstrants) against supporters of a more centralized state (Maurice, the lower classes, and the Reformed Church). As the end of the Twelve Years' Truce drew near, religious passions and the prospect of increased economic opportunity produced enthusiasm for renewed war, an enthusiasm not shared by the Remonstrants. Oldenbarnevelt actually raised troops against Maurice and the Counter Remonstrants, giving Maurice the opportunity to take him down. Oldenbarnevelt was brought to trial before a kangaroo court, convicted of treason, and beheaded.

During the trial, a national synod was called to the city of Dort (1618–1619). The synod attracted theologians from Calvinist churches around Europe—including Germany, England, Scotland, the Palatinate, and Switzerland—and was thus the closest thing to an international Calvinist synod ever held. The synod rejected Arminianism, instead opting for what became known as the Five Points of Calvinism. These are best remembered using the acronym TULIP:

- *Total depravity.* Sin affects every area of our lives to such an extent that we are effectively incapable of responding to God's grace on our own.

- *Unconditional election.* God chooses us despite ourselves and not because of anything in us, on the basis of his own sovereignty, not foreseen faith or any merits of our own.

- *Limited atonement.* Although Christ's death is sufficient to cover the sins of the entire world, in practice, its effectiveness is limited to those whom God has called to salvation; both parts of this are in accordance with God's intent for the atonement.

- *Irresistible grace.* When God calls you to salvation, he works in your life in such a way that you *will* respond.

- *Perseverance of the saints.* When you are called by God to salvation, he will continue to preserve you and keep you from falling so far that you lose your salvation.

The Canons (i.e., decrees) of Dort were tremendously controversial. The Remonstrants and some recent scholars have challenged their faithfulness to Calvin himself, since he never spoke in these terms. On the other hand, he also was never challenged on these specific issues, and I think he would have agreed with the conclusions reached by the synod. More generally, however, the synod once again pushed the issue of predestination to the forefront of Calvinist theology. This reinforced the tendency to view Calvin's thought as centered on that doctrine, which as we have seen was not the case. Even labeling the TULIP the "Five Points of Calvinism" is misleading, since even if they are faithful to Calvin's theology, the focus of his ministry was elsewhere. That said, however, the Canons of Dort became the basis of Dutch Reformed theology and had an enormous influence on international Calvinism. The Remonstrants, meanwhile, continued to protest the synod's decisions and grew progressively more rationalistic and theologically liberal as time went on, even welcoming Socinians (anti-Trinitarian precursors to Unitarians) into their seminaries.

Questions for Discussion

1. When Charles V fought the Schmalkaldic War to bring religious unity within the empire, he was willing to work with Protestant princes to try to achieve his aims. Why do you think his son Philip II was so adamantly opposed to any compromise or cooperation with Protestants in his territories?

2. The Dutch tried to develop alliances with Catholic France and Protestant England to oppose Spain, yet the trigger point for the revolt had been Philip's religious policies. Do you think the Dutch revolt was primarily about religion or politics? Why? Was Philip II right that religion and politics could not be separated, even from the point of view of the rebels?

3. What do you think of the TULIP? Which point or points do you agree with? Which do you disagree with? Why?

CHAPTER ELEVEN

The Reformation in England and Scotland

Like so much else in British history, the English and Scottish Reformations interacted with events on the Continent but really developed with an internal logic all their own. To understand the way the Reformation played out, we need to start with late-fifteenth and early-sixteenth-century dynastic politics.

Spain and England

During the late fifteenth century, the territory that would become Spain was divided up into a number of territories. The two most important were Aragon, led by its king Ferdinand, and Castile, led by its queen Isabella. Each of these kingdoms owned other territories outside of Iberia, but for our purposes in this chapter that is not terribly important. Ferdinand and Isabella decided to marry and to pass down a united kingdom to their heir. This happened to be their grandson, Charles I/V Habsburg, whom we discussed earlier. In addition to Joan the Mad, Charles's mother, Ferdinand and Isabella had another daughter, Catherine of Aragon.

With the end of the Wars of the Roses, Henry VII Tudor came to the throne of England. Spain was emerging as a great power and rival on the continent to France. Since England and France also had a longstanding rivalry, it made sense for England to set up an alliance with Spain. So, following the normal diplomatic procedures of the day, they arranged a marriage between Catherine of Aragon and Arthur, Henry VII's oldest son. Arthur, however, died shortly after the marriage. This left England and Spain in a bit of a bind; all the reasons for having the marriage were still in place, but it was illegal for Henry VII's second son, also named Henry, to marry Catherine since she was his brother's widow. Catherine, however, swore that the marriage had never been consummated, so that gave Henry VII a loophole, though canon law still said the marriage to Arthur was binding. But being king gives you clout in high places, and so the pope gave Henry special dispensation to marry Catherine. Meanwhile, Henry VII died, leaving Henry VIII on the English throne.

Henry VIII's Character

Henry was an interesting and complex character. He was a poet, musician, and patron of humanistic scholarship. He was very well educated himself—for example, he actually wrote a theological treatise refuting Luther, for which he was given the title "Defender of the Faith" by the pope. (Some people think this piece was ghostwritten by Thomas More, Henry's close friend at the time. There is no real evidence that that was the case, and Henry was certainly capable of writing it. Just because the current royal family could not write a treatise on anything doesn't mean Henry couldn't.) But this was only one side of Henry's personality. There is a technical term for the other side: He was a macho dude. He was a big, burly man who liked to show off how strong he was. To impress visiting dignitaries, Henry used to have horses brought into the throne room, which he would then wrestle to the ground. And like all macho dudes, he wanted to have sons. Lots of sons. "Big, strapping boys! Like me!" as Gaston says in Disney's *Beauty and the Beast*. So when Catherine got pregnant, there was much rejoicing. She gave birth to a child, and they named it Mary. She did get pregnant a few more times, but the children never came to term. Henry was sure that God was punishing him for his sins, and specifically for marrying his brother's widow, by not giving him sons.

Like other macho dudes, Henry also had a roving eye, and as king he felt free to indulge himself. He was having an affair with one of the daughters of the Boleyn family, when his eye fell on her younger sister Anne. He decided he wanted to have an affair with her, but she refused unless he married her. This, of course, was a problem, since he was already married to Catherine.

The King's Great Matter

The combination of disappointment at not having a son and lust for Anne was too much for Henry, and it certainly in his mind outweighed the diplomatic reasons for the marriage. So he sent his chancellor, a cardinal in the Catholic Church named Wolsey, to go to the pope to annul the marriage on grounds of consanguinity, since she was his brother's widow. (Of course, this argument conveniently ignored the fact that Henry had received a special papal dispensation to marry Catherine in the first place.) Normally, this would not have been much of a problem, except there was an additional complication at this point. The pope had gotten into a war with the Holy Roman Emperor, with the net result that imperial forces had captured Rome, making Pope Clement VII the "guest" of Charles V. Clement was thus in no position to annul Henry's marriage to Charles's aunt, and so Wolsey was sent home empty handed, ending his career in disgrace.

At this point, with Henry desperate to get out of his marriage, a man by the name of Thomas Cromwell came onto the scene. Cromwell presented a historical argument that the pope had no legitimate authority over the English church. He argued that after the Romans were driven out, Christianity had reentered Britain from Ireland, whose church was not under papal authority at the time. Only with the Synod of Whitby (664) did England abandon her allegiance to the Celtic church in favor of Rome. That was a mistake, Cromwell argued, and permitted Rome to usurp the legitimate authority of the English king over the English church. That argument was good enough for Henry, and he declared himself the head of the Church of England, divorced Catherine, and secretly married Anne, making the marriage public some time later. Cromwell became Lord Chancellor.

Henry was at best a reluctant Protestant. He took advantage of the change to close the monasteries and confiscate their property in the kingdom, yet in general his preference was to stay Catholic in every way possible, except with himself as head of the church. He savagely prosecuted and executed for treason anyone who expressed any doubts about his divorce, but at the same time he also executed mainstream Protestants as heretics. When he was in a reforming mood, he tended toward Lutheranism as less extreme than Reformed Protestantism, but he would inevitably lurch toward Catholicism pretty quickly, turning his back on reforms he had only recently instituted. His heart just wasn't in it. But it wasn't his heart that was driving his religious policy. This resulted in a wave of Protestants, known as the Henrican exiles, leaving the kingdom, typically heading toward Reformed territories on the Continent.

Second Verse, . . . a Little Bit Worse

Anne got pregnant, and there was much rejoicing. She had a baby, and they named it Elizabeth. At that point, barring another pregnancy, Anne's days were numbered. She did get pregnant, but failed to carry the child to term. So Cromwell stepped in once more. He arrested a few people, one of them a young lutenist, and tortured them into admitting to having an affair with Anne. She denied it, but her fate was pretty much sealed. Apparently, Henry offered to let her live if she agreed to an annulment; she refused, because that would have made Elizabeth illegitimate and thus ineligible for the throne. So she was condemned to be executed. Anne requested that a French headsman do the job. There were two reasons for this. First, English headsmen were not professionals—one was the town butcher, for example—and they had a very bad track record in terms of accuracy. What you don't want to happen when you're being beheaded is for the headsman to miss. Second, the French used swords rather than axes. This meant that you knelt with your head high, and the swordsman took your head off with a single horizontal swipe. With an axe, you put your head down on a chopping block. Anne wasn't about to bow her head to anyone, so she decided to go with the sword instead.

Henry's next wife was Jane Seymour. She got pregnant, and there was much rejoicing. She gave birth to a baby named Edward. So Henry had a son at last. Unfortunately, Jane died in childbirth. But Henry had his son and heir, and that was what was important to him.

Cromwell decided that England needed to develop closer ties with Protestants on the Continent and to get involved in a developing anti-Habsburg alliance, so he proposed a marriage between Anne of Cleves and Henry. Cromwell showed Henry a portrait of Anne, and Henry decided right then and there that he could marry her all right. As it turned out, however, Henry found out when Anne arrived that the portrait was unrealistically flattering. Anne was pretty full-figured, but Henry's tastes ran toward the slender and waiflike. But he had agreed to the marriage, so he more-or-less went through with it, though by all accounts he never consummated it. In fact, he referred to Anne as his "mare of Flanders." Henry ended up pressuring her into a divorce, allowing her the title of "king's sister," and beheaded Cromwell for treason.

Henry's next marriage was to Catherine Howard. Suffice it to say, she was a pretty young thing, but not terribly bright. She was caught having an affair and beheaded.

Henry's last marriage was to Catherine Parr. By this point, Henry wanted a companion more than a bed-warmer, and Catherine fit the bill well. She took care of him as well as his children, and ended up outliving Henry.

The easiest way to remember the fate of Henry's wives is through a rhyme: "Divorced, beheaded, died; divorced, beheaded, survived." And for the names, when all else fails, try Catherine; if that's not right, go with Anne.

Edward VI and Cranmer

When Henry died, he was succeeded by Edward. Edward has had a reputation for being sickly all his life, though recent research suggests he was actually quite robust. But he was a minor, so his brief reign was dominated by various factions seeking to control him. For our purposes, all we need to note about him is that he was a strident Protestant who inherited the ruthless, cold-blooded side of his family, though given his age, Tudor stubbornness comes across more as petulance.

The Church of England at this time was largely directed by Thomas Cranmer, archbishop of Canterbury. Cranmer, whose theology had moved more and more toward Reformed Protestantism, had to tread carefully during Henry's day. Now, with Edward an enthusiastic supporter of Protestantism and a minor to boot, Cranmer could work actively to shape the direction of the English church. For example, he introduced a new prayer book influenced by Reformed theology, and when the city of Strasbourg converted to Lutheranism (for political reasons) and exiled Martin Bucer, Cranmer invited him to England and gave him a professorship at Cambridge. Cranmer was supported in his work by the return of the Henrican exiles, who shared his growing enthusiasm for Reformed theology. In many ways, Cranmer is responsible for the beginnings of a distinctively English church. Unfortunately, however, it didn't last.

Bloody Mary

Just before Edward died—apparently from an infection in the chest—he tried to exclude Catholics and both of his sisters from the succession since they were not only female, but each had been declared illegitimate by separate acts of Parliament. Instead, he was pressured into naming Lady Jane Grey as his successor in his will. Lady Jane was the daughter-in-law of the duke of Northumberland, who really ran the show in Edward's last years. Edward died right after bellowing at Cranmer to witness the will. Lady Jane didn't want the office, but eventually gave in. The people, however, wouldn't accept her. Mary was the obvious alternative, and she consolidated her support quickly. Northumberland was executed, and Lady Jane and her husband were convicted of treason. Mary was unwilling to execute them, however, until a revolt raised by Lady Jane's in-laws convinced Mary that it was too dangerous to keep her and her husband alive. They were beheaded in the Tower.

Mary looked to her cousin Charles V for guidance in her early days, and she decided to marry his son and principal heir, Philip II of Spain. This was a mistake; not only were the Spanish unpopular in England—so much so that Philip left for the Continent three months after the marriage— but Spain and France were at war at this time. Although England was officially supposed to be neutral, France did its best to disrupt Mary's rule. Eventually open war broke out, and France captured Calais, the last English stronghold on the Continent.

Although Mary did not begin her reign by slaughtering her political rivals, she was less reluctant about executing other people. Given that Henry had split with Rome so he could divorce Mary's mother, Mary didn't exactly have warm feelings toward Protestantism. So she began to arrest, prosecute, and burn alive any Protestants she found, particularly clergy and other leaders. This earned her the nickname "Bloody Mary," making her the only English monarch with a mixed drink named after her. The renewed persecution caused a new wave of exiles to leave the country, known as the Marian exiles. Many of these made their way to Geneva and learned Calvin's more radical approach to Reformed theology and practice.

One of the better known of the Marian exiles was John Knox, the founder of the Church of Scotland (i.e., the Presbyterian Church). Knox, a former priest turned Protestant, had been a popular preacher in Edward's day, but when Mary Tudor came to the throne, he fled to Geneva. At this time, Scotland was ruled by Mary Guise, a rather decadent woman who was very pro-Catholic. France was believed to be ruled behind the scenes by Catherine de Medici, Henri II's wife and Mary Queen of Scots's mother-in-law; and, of course, Mary Tudor was on the throne of England. All three of these women were Catholic and encouraged—or so it was thought—the persecution and murder of Protestants. Knox decided to write a piece attacking them. His real issue was religion, but instead of focusing on that, he decided to focus on the fact that the three biggest persecutors of "true" Christians were all women. So he wrote a piece entitled *The First Blast of the Trumpet against the Monstrous Regiment of Women* (1556). He showed it to Calvin, who strongly advised against printing it; Knox, however, decided it was good, so he published it anyway. Keep that in mind—we'll return to it later.

The best-known victim of Mary's persecutions was Cranmer. When Mary came to the throne, Cranmer knew he was in trouble, so he hastily wrote up a recantation, saying he was only following the religious policies of his king, and that in his heart, he had always been a loyal Catholic. Mary thanked him for the recantation, but sentenced him to death anyway. At that point, Cranmer's resolve stiffened, and he told Mary that since he was going to die regardless,

he wanted to withdraw his recantation. He believed what he had written, and only recanted out of cowardice. He did reject the authority of Rome, he did accept Protestant doctrine, and to show his sincerity, the hand that signed the recantation would be the first thing to burn. And he was good to his word; when they chained him to the stake and lit the fire, Cranmer stretched his right hand into the flames without uttering a sound until it burned off, then he relaxed and died.

Cranmer's gruesome death turned what should have been a public relations triumph (Cranmer's recantation) into a fiasco. Cranmer's undeniable courage made him an instant hero and martyr to the Protestants and made Mary look like a tyrant. But this reversal was in many ways typical of Mary's reign. She had a reverse Midas touch—whatever she touched inevitably turned into a disaster. She wanted to turn England back to Catholicism, but not the Catholicism of the sixteenth century and the Council of Trent. Instead, she had an almost medieval notion of the church that was seriously out of date and out of touch with both the Catholic Church and the people of Britain. She and Philip had serious disagreements over religious policy. Of course, they lived in separate countries so they didn't actually see each other much. Mary also got into a war with the pope during her reign, and refused to allow the Jesuits to work within her kingdom. On a political level, she lost Calais to the French. A series of epidemics swept the kingdom, killing many. In the end, Mary simply lost her will to live. She had always had health problems, and she eventually stopped fighting them and died after preparing a will to try to ensure England's continued fidelity to Catholicism, and urging her unnamed successor to carry out her desires.

Elizabeth I Tudor

With Mary's death, the succession became a very tricky issue. From a Catholic perspective, Elizabeth was illegitimate and thus ineligible for the throne; further, she had been declared illegitimate by an act of Parliament. (Then again, so had Mary.) What this means is that Mary's death ended the Tudor line, and the throne should rightly pass to her nearest relative, Mary Queen of Scots, who by happy coincidence was also Catholic. On the other hand, Mary Queen of Scots wasn't very popular in England; people preferred the Tudor line to continue and Elizabeth to take the throne. So despite the potential legal impediments, Elizabeth became queen of England.

This didn't settle the religious question, however. There were overtures to Elizabeth from various Catholic powers assuring her that if she were to become Catholic, the pope would grant her a dispensation to rule and there would be no question of her right to the throne. On the other hand, her claim to legitimacy could be made much more easily as a Protestant, without incurring political debts to foreign powers; further, she could count on the support of the Marian exiles, which included some of the best-educated people in England. Besides, Daddy became a Protestant so he could marry Mommy. So Elizabeth reinstated Protestantism in England, and the Marian exiles came home. Among others, this included John Knox. Although he was a Scot, Knox's greatest ambition was to be an English reformer, something many Scots wish he had actually achieved. There was a minor problem, however: *The First Blast of the Trumpet against the Monstrous Regiment of Women* attacked women rulers in general, not just tyrannical or Catholic women. Elizabeth was well aware of the piece, and Knox tripped all over himself trying to apologize for it. Elizabeth never did forgive him, and so Knox's greatest impact was to be in Scotland.

Mary Queen of Scots

Elizabeth's principal concern was securing her throne, and this meant figuring out how to relate to Mary Queen of Scots. When Elizabeth came to the throne in 1558, Mary was married to the Dauphin in France. The following year, his father, Henri II, died in a jousting accident—a lance broke, and a splinter went through the eyehole of his helmet and into his brain—and the Dauphin became Francis II. He died the following year (1560), however, and shortly thereafter Mary returned to Scotland. Scotland, meanwhile, had largely converted to Protestantism, particularly the lairds, a group of Scottish nobility that had historically opposed any attempt by the monarch to rule Scotland from the center. When Mary returned, she was pressured to recognize Protestantism and to support Protestant ministers using funds from confiscated Catholic properties; over the objections of Knox, she was permitted to have her own priest and to celebrate Mass privately. The history here gets pretty complicated, with Mary accused of having multiple affairs, of ordering assassinations, and other charges. Suffice it to say, she married Henry Stewart, Lord Darnley, over the objections of the Scottish lairds. Mary became pregnant, though it was unclear who the father was; among others, it was suspected that her secretary Riccio was the father. Mary grew to hate Darnley, who suspected Riccio of turning his wife against him. So Darnley and a group of supporters seized Riccio and murdered him in front of Mary to try to cause her to miscarry; it did not work, and James VI was born in 1566. Darnley was pressured to acknowledge him as his son. Meanwhile, Mary had fallen for James Hepburn, Earl of Bothwell. Darnley got very sick, possibly from poisoning, and while he was convalescing, the house he was living in was blown up. Darnley and a page had escaped from the house prior to the explosion, however, but they were caught and strangled in the garden (1567). Suspicion immediately fell on Bothwell, whom Mary nonetheless married three months later. Opposition to this marriage was so strong that Mary was forced to abdicate in favor of James VI, who was taken from her and raised as a Presbyterian. Mary was imprisoned for a time, but in 1568 she escaped and rallied her forces in a bid to reclaim the throne. Her followers were defeated, so Mary fled to England where Elizabeth kept her under house arrest.

Elizabeth was in a difficult position. Mary was her main rival for the throne and the next in line should anything happen to her. The Catholic Church officially recognized Mary as the legitimate queen of England. And to make matters worse, the Jesuits were actively plotting to assassinate Elizabeth and put Mary on the throne. (Yes, the Jesuits were not supposed to get involved in politics. But they also had a vow of special obedience to the papacy, and in this case, that vow won out.) So Elizabeth felt forced to ban Catholic priests from the kingdom out of fear of assassination. Her very efficient secret police under Walsingham was constantly on the lookout for plots and conspiracies against Elizabeth as well. Nevertheless, Elizabeth was hesitant to act against Mary for several reasons: She was a relative; she was a monarch pushed out by her lairds, a precedent Elizabeth didn't like; and she was in the end a queen trying to run a kingdom, much like Elizabeth herself. So she kept Mary under house arrest and refused to see her, but beyond that she did nothing for nineteen years.

Foreign Policy, the Armada, and the Death of Mary Queen of Scots

Along with her internal security measures, Elizabeth used foreign policy, and specifically (potential) marital alliances, as a means to maintain her throne and to dampen potential action against her. Elizabeth was the most eligible woman in Europe, and virtually any prince of any consequence tried to court her, including Philip II, her half-sister's husband, several of his Austrian cousins, and two French princes, among others. Elizabeth strung them all along, never committing to any of them, but never saying "no" either. This kept England at peace for a fair period of time, since no one wanted to lose his chance to win her.

At the same time, however, she did support the rebels in the Spanish Netherlands who were fighting for their independence from Spain (see chapter 10), and she permitted her "privateers" (essentially licensed pirates) to raid Spanish ships and even Spanish territory while at the same time denying that they were acting according to her instructions or with her consent. Philip eventually caught on to the fact that Elizabeth wasn't going to marry him (or any other Catholic), and her support for the Dutch rebels and the privateers meant that she had to go. As a result, he began to assemble the largest naval force known to history at that time, the Armada, intending it to ferry troops from the Netherlands to England for an invasion, backed by a presumed uprising of English supporters of Mary Queen of Scots.

With the preparations for the Armada under way, Elizabeth faced a number of dilemmas. Parliament argued that the Spanish plans could only succeed with the help of Mary, either as a potential "native" queen (she was Henry VIII's great-granddaughter) or at the head of a Catholic rebellion; thus, the safest thing to do would be to execute Mary. Elizabeth refused, but Mary forced her hand. She had been corresponding in code with some Catholics in the kingdom and became involved in a plot to assassinate Elizabeth. Walsingham's men had cracked the code, however, and thus the entire conspiracy was unmasked. She was put on trial and convicted; her coconspirators were executed, but Elizabeth delayed signing the order for Mary's execution for three months. Eventually, Elizabeth was apparently tricked into signing it, and Mary was beheaded in February 1587.

The execution outraged Philip, making him more determined than ever to bring Elizabeth down. Unfortunately, however, almost everything that could have gone wrong did. Sir Francis Drake raided Cadiz and burned the supply of seasoned wood for barrel staves. The barrels made to hold water for the Armada thus were made of green wood, making them leaky and fouling the drinking water. The admiral kept the troops on the ships for days prior to departure, so they consumed a significant percentage of the provisions before they ever set off. Philip didn't allow his admiral and his general in the Netherlands to communicate directly with each other, but only through Philip himself. As a result, the planning and coordination went seriously wrong. And all that was before they actually set sail for England.

For her part, Elizabeth called her privateers back and mobilized the country. She appeared before the troops in armor, calling on them to defend her honor and that of England. It was, by all accounts, a rousing speech. When the Armada was spotted, the English attacked in smaller, faster, more maneuverable ships with better cannons. Although it wasn't a decisive victory, the English did get the better of the Armada. Nonetheless, the Armada got through, but when the Spanish reached the Netherlands, they got a nasty shock: The ships had too deep a draft to make it to the harbors, and there were no boats available to ferry the troops out to them, a result of the communications failures between the admiral and the general. Then the weather turned against them, and the Spanish lost more men and ships to the storms than to English guns. Suffice it to say, the Armada ended as a disaster for Spain. The battle was a tremendous victory for Elizabeth and England, though in one of the more dishonorable elements of her reign, after her victory Elizabeth left her sailors in inadequate shelters on the coast through the winter; she refused to pay them or to provide food or medical care for the many who got sick. She always was something of a cheapskate, and in this case, it killed many of the sailors who had fought for her.

Religious Policy and the Elizabethan Settlement

The Armada was the last major challenge to Elizabeth's reign. There were other issues she needed to deal with, however. Although the main threat to her throne came from Catholicism, Elizabeth also cordially detested the Calvinists. Her tastes ran toward Catholic-style rituals, pomp and ceremony, though she seems to have had little real interest in religion. She claimed that she subscribed to the Augsburg Confession, though there were very few Lutherans in her kingdom. My guess is that her verbal adherence to the Augsburg Confession was dictated by political considerations rather than religious conviction; in 1555, it had been accepted as a legitimate creed in the Holy Roman Empire, so even the Habsburgs recognized that it had some legitimacy. Lutherans governed the church via bishops, which was more compatible with monarchy than the Reformed tendency to use representative councils

to run the churches (see chapter 12); Lutherans also detested Calvinists. Whatever her views, she emphatically did not want the Calvinists to gain the upper hand in the church. They were too austere, too fanatical, too dangerous to the political order generally. On the other hand, a significant percentage of her theologians, pastors, and educated laity were Reformed and had been since the days of Cranmer; a very vocal group were out-and-out Calvinists as well. So Elizabeth instituted a religious policy known as the Elizabethan Settlement that combined a moderate Calvinism (how's that for an oxymoron?) with Catholic-style pomp and ceremony. On the surface, this looks like an attempt at compromise, but in reality it was intended to undercut the influence of the Calvinists in the Church of England; all churches in England were to use exactly the same practices and liturgy, leaving no room for the far more austere, preaching-oriented services of Calvin's Geneva.

For their part, the Calvinists protested against many of the practices Elizabeth enforced in the churches. The first big controversy involved vestments; pastors had to wear all the accoutrements of Catholic priests. The Calvinists argued that this was a return to papist superstition and idolatry; the Church of England responded that it was biblical, since the priests in the Old Testament also wore vestments. The Calvinists responded that becoming Judaizers was not much better than being papal idolators. The Church of England then argued that since the New Testament does not discuss vestments, it's *adiaphora*, that is, an "indifferent" matter that Christians can differ on; thus, the church could mandate that they be worn without violating Scripture. The Calvinists responded that if it was an indifferent matter, then the church could not insist on it. And so on. Suffice it to say, the controversy eventually died down and Anglican pastors wore vestments. But the Vestment Controversy was the opening salvo in a protracted conflict over the nature of the Anglican Church. The Calvinists thought Elizabeth's reforms did not go far enough to purify the church from abuses, and thus they became known as "Puritans." Although the Puritans would not raise any other major controversies during Elizabeth's reign once the vestment issue was settled, they would be considerably more troublesome under her successors.

This does not mean that the Puritans were uninvolved in Elizabethan life, however. Popular pictures of the period tend to focus on the Elizabethan Renaissance, on Shakespeare and Marlow, on Purcell, on Spenser, on theatre, music, and poetry. Anybody with any sense spent their spare time at the Globe Theatre. Puritans, if they appear at all, are seen as a bunch of religious fanatics and killjoys, nutcases on the margins of society that no one takes particularly seriously. In murder mysteries set in Elizabethan England, they're usually the psychotic killers. We get this picture because the people who write the books and movies about the period tend to be English majors who really like Shakespeare. Unfortunately, this is not an accurate picture of the place of Puritans (or the arts) in Elizabethan life. Far from being marginal religious fanatics, the Puritans were among the best educated and most successful people in England. Cambridge University became a bastion of Puritan thought; the movers and shakers in the economy were frequently Puritan sympathizers; Puritan lectureships were as popular as theatre among the educated classes; eventually, Puritan leadership in their communities enabled them to take over the House of Commons in Parliament. All this is hardly the work of fringe religious nuts. In fact, among the book buying public, Puritans were far and away the most popular authors of the day; any of about a dozen

Puritan divines single-handedly outsold the combined production of the entire Elizabethan Renaissance.

When Elizabeth died, she willed the throne to James VI of Scotland, the son of Mary Queen of Scots. James VI thus became James I of England and the first of the Stuart line. The story of the Stuarts belongs to a different book, however, though James and his daughter Elizabeth will put in a brief appearance in chapter 13. In the meantime, we need to cross the channel and look at the Reformation in France.

Questions for Discussion

1. Henry VIII is a larger-than-life figure in many ways. What do you think of him? Which of his wives do you find most interesting? Why?
2. Discuss the interaction between religion, family interests, and politics during the reigns of Henry's children. Are there any new dimensions that we haven't seen in previous chapters dealing with politics and religion?
3. Did the popularity of the Puritans in England come as a surprise to you?
4. What do you think of the Elizabethan Settlement? Was it a viable program for the long term? Why do you think it worked even temporarily in the face of Puritan opposition?

CHAPTER TWELVE

The Reformation in France

French Catholicism

France had always been a very Catholic country. Its king was considered a quasi-sacred figure, the descendant of Clovis, first of the barbarian kings to accept orthodox Christianity. French kings celebrated Mass on their coronation, the only laypersons to do so, and were believed to have the power to cure scrofula (tuberculosis of the lymph glands, especially in the neck) by the laying on of hands. If they were always a bit independent of Rome—insisting, for example, on the right to appoint their own bishops—they nonetheless saw it as their duty to suppress heresy in the kingdom, a duty that figured prominently in their coronation oaths. Heresy had historically been a problem, particularly in the southern parts of the kingdom where Albigensianism had flourished in the late twelfth and early thirteenth centuries, but this had led the University of Paris to emerge as the most prominent theological school in Europe. The Sorbonne, as the theological faculty was frequently called, was a bastion of the scholastic approach to theology. Although they did not always support papal prerogatives, they were methodologically conservative and stuck very closely to medieval theological formulations. The people of France too had strong ties to traditional Catholicism, particularly during the Reformation. Popular religion was dominated by a fixation on prophecy, omens, signs and wonders, astrology—the kind of things supermarket tabloids peddle today. They were especially concerned about portents of the coming of the antichrist and divine judgment, particularly with the rise of Protestantism, which they saw as confirmation that the apocalypse was at hand.

Early Reform and Crackdowns

At the same time, there were progressive elements within the French church. Humanism was a growing movement among French intellectuals, as we have seen in our discussion of Calvin. French humanists tended to focus particularly on societal reform, which in the case of France meant of necessity church reform, so most early French humanists were involved in trying to clean up the problems in the church. For example, Lefèvre d'Etaples wrote a number of important biblical commentaries (including one that talked about justification by faith several years before Luther did) and worked with his protégé Guillaume Briçonnet to reform first the monastery of St. Germain-des-Près outside of Paris where Briçonnet was abbot, and then the diocese of Meaux when Briçonnet became bishop there. The Meaux circle included among others Guillaume Farel, who would later pressure Calvin into staying in Geneva. Similarly Marguerite of Angoulême, the queen of Navarre and sister of Francis I, king of France, was also heavily involved with the *évangeliques,* the reform party within the Catholic Church that wanted to see more emphasis on the gospel and a progressive (i.e., humanistic) approach to religion. More broadly, small circles of *évangeliques* and Protestants began to develop across France. It seems that this was initially an urban movement centered in the educated, fairly affluent crafts and professions. There is an exception to every generalization about the makeup of these groups, though: They were urban, except in the Cévennes where they were rural; they included wealthier, educated professionals, except in Amiens where they included almost exclusively uneducated, poor textile workers, and so on. As long as these groups remained confined primarily to relatively elite groups in society, they were generally ignored by the authorities; once they started spreading to the masses, however, the authorities began to get worried. Ultimately, these cells included members from every segment of society from nobility to peasants, and that's when the trouble started.

Several other things went wrong for the reformers almost simultaneously. First, the Sorbonne did not want the humanists, who were not formally trained in theology, messing with their turf. They did not like Erasmus, Lefèvre, and a host of other humanist reformers, and wanted to see them tried for heresy. Second, Luther's ideas were beginning to spread in France, and by the 1520s the Sorbonne and the *parlements* (royal law courts) were determined to drive them out. Third, and even worse, some people were beginning to adopt sacramentarian ideas as well. As we saw in chapter 5, "sacramentarians" rejected the presence of Christ's body and blood in the bread and wine. Oddly enough, this was a bigger deal in France than justification by faith was. The French thought of power as being a single thing that could be applied in different spheres of life. With transubstantiation, we see an example of power being embodied in physical elements. This provided a metaphor for all sorts of power in society. It explained why the king and the government had authority, why the social structure was set up the way it was, why some groups had privileges and rights that others didn't, and so on. Attacking transubstantiation thus undermined the underlying picture that was used to explain the entire society; sacramentarians were thus seen as anarchists and inherently dangerous to the realm. Unfortunately for Lefèvre and Briçonnet, sacramentarian ideas were beginning to surface in Meaux. When the *parlements* and the Sorbonne began their crackdown on "heresy," they squashed the reform at Meaux; to avoid becoming the guest of honor at a public barbeque, Lefévre fled to Marguerite of Angoulême, who shielded him and other humanist and Protestant reformers from persecution.

Francis I was not as concerned about the reformers as the Sorbonne and *Parlement* of Paris were, at least until 1534. Protestant pastor Antoine Marcourt had written a broadside attacking transubstantiation as idolatry and the concept of the sacrifice of the Mass as blasphemy. In October, these were posted simultaneously in Paris, Noyon, Tours, Orléans, Rouen, Blois—and even on the door to Francis I's bedchamber. Francis was furious. He ordered the arrest, trial, and execution of the heretics. When further sacramentarian writings were discovered at the Louvre palace and elsewhere in Paris, he began an even more systematic crackdown on Protestantism and participated in a Corpus Christi procession to show his support for transubstantiation. He and his successors would continue sporadic persecution of Protestants for decades to come.

The Development of the French Reformed Church

Despite the persecution, Protestantism spread quickly across the country. No one is really sure why, though there have been numerous theories offered ranging from economic crises, to social forces, to an attempt to escape from the "prophetic anguish" of popular Catholicism to a more rational form of religion. What is clear is that this was a very dynamic time for Protestantism in the kingdom. The persecution itself contributed to this; since Protestantism was forced underground into relatively isolated cells, it took a bewildering array of forms in terms of both doctrine and organization. Lucien Fèbvre described it as a period of "magnificent religious anarchy." This in itself probably contributed to the growth, as *évangeliques* and Protestant ideas mutated to fit the interests, preferences, circumstances, and temperaments of the individuals involved in the groups. By the 1540s, however, the character of French Protestantism began to change. Calvin began publishing theological works in French, the first time that serious theological works were available in the language. This began to shift the doctrinal center of gravity among the kingdom's Protestants toward Geneva and its expatriate French theologian. The shift toward Calvinism was accelerated in the 1550s, as Geneva began to send missionary pastors to France to found and head churches throughout the kingdom.

The 1550s saw another shift as increasing numbers of the nobility converted to Protestantism, including a number of the Princes of the Blood (i.e., members of the extended royal family). This gave French Protestants protectors with enough political and military clout to force the monarchy to take them seriously. Noblemen sponsored churches in cities and on their rural estates, protected Protestants as they met to sing psalms or hear sermons, and generally supported the growth of the movement in the kingdom. But at the same time, they also shifted the center of gravity for French Protestantism away from the nonnoble, urban churches that still formed the numerical majority of Protestants in the kingdom toward the rural estates of the nobility. The conversion of the nobility also changed something of the ethos of the Huguenots (i.e., French Protestants). Traditionally, Huguenot piety had been built around a strict moral code focused on submission to the laws of God and the magistrate; nobles, by contrast, saw themselves as a privileged class with special rights and prerogatives, and conversion to Protestantism didn't change this. This attitude would have disastrous results for the Protestants. For example, the *Conjuration d'Amboise,* a botched attempt to kidnap the king (who was a minor at the time) in order to "free him" from the influence of the "evil advisors" on the regency council, resulted in the capture and execution of a number of Protestant noblemen.

By the late 1550s, a number of the pastors in the kingdom decided it was high time to get organized. In a meeting held secretly in Paris in 1559, they adopted a confession of faith known as the Gallican Confession and a church order known as the Ecclesiastical Discipline. The Gallican Confession, which was based on the statement of faith of the Reformed Church of Paris, became a model for the Belgic Confession of the Dutch Reformed Church and influenced other later confessions. The Discipline had an even bigger impact. The challenge that faced the

emerging French Reformed Church was simple: How do you take churches that had been independent and bring them into a single ecclesiastical organization? Every system that had been set up prior to this was inherently hierarchical, giving to certain members of the clergy (i.e., bishops) or to certain churches rights over other clergy and churches. Unfortunately, this approach wouldn't work in this case. Churches that had previously been independent were unlikely to willingly place themselves under the authority of another church—especially French churches. At the same time, no church could be permitted to make a decision that affected another church without that church having a say in it, since otherwise the church that made the decision unilaterally would effectively be claiming authority over the other. To solve the problem, the Discipline developed a system to allow local churches autonomy over their own affairs while developing a non-hierarchical system for resolving "matters of mutual interest." Local churches were governed by a consistory much like Geneva's, except these consistories included the deacons and were to oversee all aspects of the church's life. The churches were to send representatives to a regional meeting known as the colloquy, and to a provincewide meeting known as the provincial synod. The provincial synods sent representatives to the national synod. The idea was to keep decision making on as local a level as possible, and only to bring issues that involved multiple churches or appeals of disciplinary decisions to the colloquies or synods. Although the system was designed to meet the peculiar situation facing French Protestants, it proved to be a very powerful and flexible system. It was adopted (and adapted) by the Dutch Reformed Church and eventually by the Presbyterian Church as well, though for very different reasons in each case: The representative system fit the governmental structure of the Dutch Republic, and in Scotland the presbyteries (=colloquies) were controlled by the lairds, who used them to counterbalance the power of the king.

Royal Politics

The year 1559 also saw the death of Henri II, Francis I's son and successor, in a jousting accident. He was succeeded by his son, Francis II, who was married to Mary Queen of Scots. Francis was weak in body and will, and his court soon became dominated by the Guise family, Mary's maternal relatives from Lorraine in northeastern France. The Guises were rivals to Gaspard de Coligny, a Prince of the Blood and the effective leader of the Huguenot party, though by birth the young Henri de Bourbon, king of Navarre, actually outranked him. The Guises were also moving on the road toward ultra-Catholicism, though they were not quite there yet; they had already developed a strong hatred of the Huguenots, however. Francis II showed every sign of continuing or accelerating Francis I's and Henri II's policy of persecution of Protestants, but before he could do so, he died. So in 1560, he was succeeded by his next brother, Charles IX, and Guise influence at court waned.

At this point, we need to discuss the queen mother, Catherine de Medici. Catherine had a great deal of influence at court; in fact, she seems to have done more to run the country than her sons did except during the Guise ascendancy under Francis II. Catherine has traditionally been portrayed as a manipulative, evil puppet master, controlling everything that happened at court from behind the scenes, dominating her sons and pushing through her nefarious schemes with a ruthlessness that would have done Machiavelli proud. This picture of Catherine is a serious distortion. Yes, she did have an excessive amount of influence on her sons. Yes, she did set much of the royal policy in conjunction with her moderate chancellor, Michel de l'Hôpital. Yes, she even had a court sorcerer who advised her. But her policy was guided throughout by the simple desire to preserve the kingdom for her sons. As she watched France slip toward civil war over religion, she did everything in her power to prevent the chaos that could cost her sons their kingdom or even their lives. She sponsored a religious discussion, the Colloquy of Poissy, between Catholics and Calvinists (including Theodore Beza, an expatriate French nobleman himself) to try to settle the religious differences. When that didn't work, she issued the Edict of January, allowing Protestant noblemen the freedom to hold worship services on their rural estates and Protestants to worship outside the major cities. This was an attempt to appease the Protestant nobility, though it didn't really address the needs of the majority of Protestants who lived in the cities—but it did advance Catherine's fundamental goal of putting a damper on religious conflict.

The Wars of Religion
and the St. Bartholomew's Day Massacres

Unfortunately, these policies were too moderate to work in an era of such religious passions. While the Guises were on their way back home from Paris early in 1562, they came upon a Protestant congregation worshiping legally in a village called Vassy. The Guises were so incensed by this that they simply slaughtered the lot of them. This led to a mobilization of forces on both sides and the first of the interminable Wars of Religion that would plague France for the rest of the century and beyond. The pattern of the wars was relatively simple:

1. War would start.
2. The two sides would fight to a standstill.
3. A peace would be set up granting the Protestants more or less rights than they had before depending on how well they did on the battlefield.
4. The peace would stick for a little while, then one side (frequently the Guises) would break the truce and another war would start.
5. Repeat as necessary.

This was almost exactly what Catherine had been trying to avoid, so she decided to try to make peace using the traditional means of a marital alliance. She arranged a wedding between her daughter Marguerite and Henri of Navarre, the titular head of the Protestant side. The Huguenots were given a safe-conduct to Paris for the wedding in August 1572. At this point, Charles IX was very much under the influence of Admiral Coligny, the real leader of the Huguenots. Coligny was pushing Charles to back the rebellion against Spain in the Low Countries. This would address several issues: It would unite the French, Catholic and

Protestant alike, against a common enemy; it would strike a blow against the Habsburgs, who had long been rivals of the Valois; and, coincidentally, it would also aid the Protestant cause by promoting the establishment of a Protestant state. Not surprisingly, the Guises were upset by this plan, and even more by the influence Coligny had on the king. So they decided to assassinate him. Unfortunately, the assassin only wounded Coligny; the Huguenots were furious, thinking that the king (or Catherine de Medici) had lured them to the city under the pretense of a safe-conduct to murder Coligny, and maybe even the rest of them. Paris itself was tense over the arrival of the Huguenots, whom the very Catholic populace of the city saw as heretics, anarchists, traitors, and the harbingers of the antichrist.

In this atmosphere of tension and mistrust, the Royal Council held an emergency meeting. Fearing rather irrationally that the Huguenots would seize the palace and slaughter the royal family, the council decided that Coligny would have to be finished off and the story presented that he was plotting against the throne. The Guises gleefully went out to kill Coligny. When they told the guard that what they were doing was the king's will, something got misunderstood and as the bell sounded midnight on St. Bartholomew's Day, a general slaughter of the Protestants in the city ensued. Coligny was killed, his body thrown from a window, mutilated, and dragged through the streets. Thousands of others were killed as well and their bodies thrown into the Seine. Henri of Navarre abjured his faith and converted to Catholicism to save his life. When word of the events in Paris spread to other cities, copycat massacres occurred throughout the kingdom. No one knows the death toll of the St. Bartholomew's Day Massacres, though 20,000 seems a reasonable guess. When word reached Rome, the pope ordered a Te Deum sung to celebrate.

The massacres had profound effects on French Protestants. Many converted back to Catholicism, seeing this as the judgment of God, and as a result the momentum the Protestant side had been building was decisively broken. That didn't mean they went away, however. The older, politically savvy leadership had all been slaughtered, and a new generation of hotheads rose to positions of leadership in the movement. The Huguenots could no longer claim to be loyal to the king and only opposed to his evil advisors since the king openly admitted involvement in the massacres. So they began to develop a theory of political resistance based on Luther, but arguing more generally that lesser magistrates had the authority to resist even the king once he became a tyrant—and murdering thousands of your own citizens certainly qualified as tyranny. The resistance theory developed here moved step-by-step to the development of resistance theory in England, culminating in John Locke's treatises on government, and from there provided the inspiration for the American Declaration of Independence. Eventually, Henri of Navarre escaped, renounced his conversion, and took his place at the head of the Huguenots.

Many Catholics were also horrified by the massacres. A third force arose, known today as the *Politiques,* who advocated finding a political solution to the religious questions facing France. Although the king was not always in their camp, they tended to center themselves around the monarchy as the only viable alternative to anarchy.

The wars continued. Charles IX died, and was succeeded by his brother Henri III. Henri III was weaker personally than even his brothers had been. Although intelligent and a patron of the arts, he was lazy, enamored with pleasure, and given to scandalous behavior. For example, he was fond of dressing in women's clothing.

His decadence was too much for the ultra-Catholic faction headed by the Guises known as the Catholic League; they rioted against him and came close to supporting Henri de Guise for the throne. In an effort to break the power of the Guises, Henri III had Henri de Guise assassinated in 1588, turning the Catholic League definitively against the king. Spain threw its lot behind the Catholic League, and Henri III was forced to ally himself with Henri of Navarre. While the two Henris were besieging Paris, a Dominican friar slipped into the camp using false papers and assassinated Henri III. His younger brother had already died, and neither he nor any of his brothers left any legitimate children to take the throne, and thus the Valois dynasty came to an end. That meant the throne passed to a cadet line, the nearest of which was the Bourbons. So Henri de Bourbon, king of Navarre, the head of the Huguenots, became king of France, as confirmed by Henri III himself on his deathbed. Makes you wonder what the Dominican was thinking.

Henri IV and the Edict of Nantes

So Henri de Bourbon now became Henri IV. The problem was, the Catholics wouldn't accept a Huguenot king. Henri IV had a tremendous amount of military success around the country, but he did not control Paris, and he knew he could not rule France without the city. He could have starved it out or stormed it, but he didn't want to do either. Finally, he is reputed to have said, "Paris is worth a Mass," and reconverted back to Catholicism. (Actually, he probably never said that, but it does a good job of summarizing his attitude toward the situation.) The Guises cried foul and said it was a fake conversion, you couldn't trust Henri, and so on. No one listened: Paris opened its gates

to him, and Henri IV became the most popular king in French history. His first act on coming to the throne was to declare a general amnesty for the Wars of Religion; he then brought the troops on all sides together to drive out the Spanish troops who had been supporting the Catholic League. Once that was done, he went to work to craft a solution for the religious troubles in France. After some negotiations, Henri issued the Edict of Nantes in 1598. The Edict was designed to put a stop to the Wars of Religion. It provided for places of worship for the Huguenots in the country and most cities in the kingdom except Paris. Bipartisan courts were to be set up with both Catholic and Protestant justices to settle cases involving members of the two communities. In its secret provisions, it allowed the Huguenots a number of fortified cities as guarantees of the crown's good faith. And its provisions were to be kept in effect until such time as religious uniformity could be established in the kingdom.

The Edict of Nantes was an important milestone in that it was the first time a major kingdom had established a policy that permitted two confessions to live side-by-side under the same jurisdiction. But it would be a mistake to view it as introducing toleration in France. No one wanted toleration; both sides wanted to win all the marbles. And the terms of the Edict itself show that the goal was religious uniformity, not permanent religious division. What the Edict did was to regulate the terms of the debate between the two sides so that the religious issues would be settled by words and not swords.

Henri IV may have been France's most popular king, but that doesn't mean everyone loved him. In 1610 he was assassinated by a deranged ex-monk named Ravaillac, who believed Henri was planning a war against the pope. Henri IV was succeed by young son Louis XIII.

Richelieu and Absolutism

Louis XIII was a minor when he came to the throne, and he never took a very active role in running the kingdom even after he became an adult. Instead, his policy was directed primarily by Cardinal Armand Jean du Plessis de Richelieu, who became the king's chief minister in 1624. Richelieu was a political genius and was one of the driving forces behind the rise of absolutism in Europe, that is, the concept that the king is the ultimate authority in any kingdom and whatever he says, goes. This was tied to the idea of the divine right of kings, that the king is answerable to no one but God himself. Both of these represented a major shift from medieval concepts of kingship, which included explicit limitations on the king's authority. But the experience of the Wars of Religion in France and the general political climate in early seventeenth-century Europe paved the way for this newer, more centralized concept of government. (Whether absolutism existed in more than theory is another question, but that would take us too far afield to discuss here.) Richelieu's guiding principle was *raison d'état,* "reason of state," which said in essence that no one can claim special interests, rights, or prerogatives ahead of those of the crown. This naturally led Richelieu into a conflict with a wide range of privileged groups in France whose power he tried to curtail. Thus, for example, he worked to curb the power of the provincial governors and upper nobility, who treated their territories almost as independent states, by appointing officials known as *intendents* to ride herd over them. Similarly, he worked to force the Huguenots into direct dependence on the king by attacking and destroying their main stronghold at La Rochelle. And even though a cardinal in the Catholic Church, Richelieu acted against the interests of Rome by supporting the Protestants during the Thirty Years' War. We turn to that war in our concluding chapter.

Questions for Discussion

1. We have seen disputes about the Eucharist separate Catholic from Protestant and Protestant from Protestant before. Why were they particularly significant in France? What do you think of the notion of using the Eucharist as a model for the entire political and social hierarchy?

2. In light of the belief in Nostradamus's prophecies (a sixteenth-century Frenchman, by the way), UFOs, and all the superstition and pseudo-mysticism we see displayed in supermarket tabloids and elsewhere, how different do you think we are from the popular French Catholicism of the sixteenth century? Does Christianity offer a more rational view of the world?

3. What is the significance of the church structure devised

by the French Reformed Churches? In light of the connection between civil government and church government ("If it's good enough for God, it's good enough for the state"), can you see any parallels to patterns of republican government (i.e., government by representation) in Western civil governments?

4. Richelieu is best known for articulating the principle of *raison d'état,* though he was hardly the first to use it as a principle of government. Can you identify any other examples of rulers in the preceding chapters who governed using that principle, even if it had not been formally named yet?

CHAPTER THIRTEEN

The Thirty Years' War and the End of the Era

The Situation in the Empire

Many tensions were simmering just below the surface in early seventeenth-century Europe. The Habsburgs remained the dominant power on the Continent, but they were mistrusted by many of the princes within the empire as well as by the Magyars and the Slavic peoples in central Europe. Although France's dynasty had changed, the Bourbons had no more love for the Habsburgs than the Valois had had. In fact, only Henri IV's assassination in 1610 prevented an outbreak of war between the Holy Roman Emperor and an alliance of anti-Habsburg powers led by France over the succession to Jülich-Cleves; there was other near miss over the succession in Montferrat in northern Italy. Spain remained powerful militarily and wanted nothing more than to regain complete control of the Netherlands. The Dutch, meanwhile, were equally determined to remain independent, and began poaching on the Portuguese spice trade (a legitimate act of war when the Dutch began doing it, since Spain had absorbed Portugal in 1580). And religious tensions continued. Within the empire, the Religious Peace of Augsburg kept a lid on things, with one significant exception: The Palatinate had converted to Calvinism, which was illegal under the terms of the Religious Peace of Augsburg. The Palatinate was a wealthy and important territory. Its capital was Heidelberg, and it included not only the region around the capital but a discontinuous territory downriver on the Rhine. Calvinist ideas spread from the Palatinate into neighboring territories and even into Brandenburg, where it would be accepted by the Hohenzollern electors. Further, the prince of the Palatinate was one of the electors of the Holy Roman Empire and the head of the Protestant Union, the coalition that very nearly went to war with the emperor and with the Catholic League, headed by Maximilian of Bavaria, in 1609. No one was ready to make an issue of the Palatinate's religion with the ongoing threat of the Ottomans to the east, but there was nonetheless a great deal of tension beneath the surface, not only between Catholics and Protestants but between Lutherans and Calvinists as well.

In central Europe, antipathy toward Germans in general and the Habsburgs in particular translated into support for the Reformation. Protestantism initially spread via Saxon merchant communities, and frequently was not widely accepted by the non-German locals. The advent of Reformed Protestantism, however, gave the Slavs and Magyars a viable alternative to still more German (i.e., Lutheran) domination, and as a result, Calvinism spread widely in Hungary, Bohemia, and Poland. Perhaps because they were border territories, Poland and Transylvania established a remarkable degree of religious toleration for Catholics, Lutherans, Calvinists, Anabaptists, and even anti-Trinitarians. The flashpoint for the war, however, was the Czech kingdom of Bohemia.

Bohemia and the Defenestration of Prague

The situation in Bohemia was complex. Charles V had been succeeded as emperor and as lord of the Austrian Habsburg lands by his brother, Ferdinand I (1558–1564), who inherited the kingship of Bohemia and large territories in Hungary, though both of these kingdoms nominally had elective monarchies. Ferdinand was succeeded by his son Maximilian II (1564–1576). There were large Protestant minorities in Bohemia, Hungary, and Moravia, and they very nearly won Maximilian II to their side. In 1575 he granted followers of the Bohemian Confession the right to worship freely in all Czech territories (i.e., Bohemia and Moravia). The next year, the throne passed to his son Rudolf II (1576–1612). Although a devout Catholic, Rudolf didn't trust the Jesuits and hesitated to apply the provisions of the Religious Peace of Augsburg or of the Council of Trent in most of his territories. In fact, Czech resistance to both Habsburg domination and Lutheranism forced Rudolf to grant complete religious freedom in the kingdom in his Letter of Majesty (1609); he even moved his capital to Prague. It is worth noting that Rudolf's mother, Maria of Spain, was his father's first cousin. Inbreeding has its consequences, and Rudolf was noted for his eccentricities and pathological obsession with astrology. These traits caused the family to unite behind his brother Matthias, who deposed Rudolf in

1612. Matthias couldn't control the religious situation any better than his brother, however, and with the help of his advisor Melchior Khlesl continued a policy of de facto toleration of the Protestants.

In 1617, Matthias stepped down as king of Bohemia. He had always been a bit sickly (it's a shame when first cousins marry) and never had any heirs, so he pushed Ferdinand Habsburg, his cousin, as his successor. The Estates of Bohemia were controlled by Protestants, and they did not trust the Jesuit-educated Ferdinand, who had long opposed any concessions to Protestants. But the Estates did not see any practical way they could block the succession, so they approached Ferdinand with the proposal that they would not oppose his election if he would agree to uphold the Letter of Majesty and preserve their freedoms. Ferdinand agreed, and he became king of Bohemia in 1617. Almost immediately, he broke his promise and began to crack down on Protestantism. The Protestants responded by meeting together and writing a protest to the emperor about the violation of their constitution, but Matthias declared their meeting illegal and refused to act. A group of armed Protestant nobles led by Count Heinrich von Thurn responded by marching on the palace in Prague. They didn't find Ferdinand there, but they did find two of his regents and a secretary. In what amounts to a time-honored form of political protest in Bohemia, they threw the three of them out of an upper story window fifty feet down into the moat. (Yes, the Czechs had been doing that since the Middle Ages; arguably, the Communist government in Czechoslovakia was still doing it in the 1950s.) The regents and secretary got away with their lives, if not their dignity, because they landed in a pile of organic fertilizer in the moat. This event, known as the Defenestration of Prague, marked the beginning of the Thirty Years'

War. (Isn't English great? We actually have a verb that means "to throw out a window.") The Protestant Estates declared the throne vacant and began looking for a Protestant noble to take over.

The Bohemian and Palatine Phases of the War

At this point the Estates hit a snag—no Protestant elector was willing to accept the throne. First, doing so would have annoyed the Habsburgs. Second, what Ferdinand had done may have been impolitic, but it was not necessarily illegal. It set a bad precedent to allow the nobles to depose a duly elected king because they didn't like his policies. But then Matthias died, and Ferdinand was elected Holy Roman Emperor. At this point, Frederick V, the Calvinist Elector Palatine and son-in-law of James I of England, decided that since Matthias had resigned as king of Bohemia while emperor, this set a precedent. Ferdinand was now emperor, so he had de facto resigned as king of Bohemia. The throne was thus empty, and so Frederick accepted it. There were two problems with this line of reasoning. First, the precedent was far from clear; second, Ferdinand disagreed with the argument, and this gave him the excuse to come down hard not only on Bohemia but on the illegally Calvinist Palatinate. Although he was delayed by a number of uprisings against his rule, notably in Hungary, Ferdinand found a key supporter in Maximilian of Bavaria, to whom Ferdinand promised the electoral office plus a good chunk of the Palatinate. Maximilian's army, under his general Count Tilly, marched against Bohemia. Significantly, even Lutheran princes in the empire lent Ferdinand their support or sat on their hands; Calvinists were in some ways worse than Catholics, so why help them? Tilly's army delivered a smashing defeat of the Bohemians at the battle of White Mountain in 1620. Prague was plundered for a week, the landed nobles who backed Frederick were tried and executed or driven off their lands, the formerly free peasants were reenserfed, Protestants were driven out of the kingdom, and Bohemia was made a hereditary monarchy in Habsburg hands. Moravia, the other Czech state, met a similar fate.

Tilly then turned his troops to the upper Palatinate near Heidelberg. Rather than defending his territory, Frederick V was pathetically running around trying to find someone who would support his claim to Bohemia, but no one would. So Tilly sacked Heidelberg, the capital of German Calvinism, and occupied the upper Palatinate. Spanish troops from the Netherlands attacked the lower Palatinate and took it over quickly. Calvinists were driven out of the territory, followed quickly by the Lutherans. At about this point, however, the Spanish and Austrian Habsburgs had a policy split: Spain wanted Frederick V put back in charge of the Palatinate as elector since they did not want to antagonize Frederick's father-in-law, James I of England. The Twelve Years' Truce was expiring, Spain was renewing its war with the Dutch, and they wanted England neutral. Ferdinand had it in for Frederick, however, and in any event needed to keep his promises to Maximilian of Bavaria. So Maximilian became elector and was given the upper Palatinate, the lower Palatinate east of the Rhine, and parts of Bohemia; the lower Palatinate west of the Rhine was left in Spanish hands. Maximilian was thus left for the time being with power that was beginning to rival the Habsburgs. Other imperial territories also saw the opportunity to grab land from their neighbors, spurred on by the ambitions of the mercenary generals who ran their armies.

The Danish Phase

The Protestants of the empire were unhappy with this state of affairs. Even though Frederick was a Calvinist, the Lutherans did not want his electoral office falling into the hands of the Catholics, since that would upset the balance of power between Catholics and Protestants within the empire. They decided to reactivate the anti-Habsburg Protestant Union to resist the emperor, and started casting about for support. Denmark, a Lutheran state, was happy to take the leading role in the league since it had territorial ambitions in Schleswig and Holstein just south of its border. England and Scotland were willing to give some indirect support to aid Frederick (or, more precisely, to avenge the dishonor shown to his wife, Elizabeth Stuart, James I's daughter). But the Protestant states needed money to have any hope of success. Catholic France was happy to supply this under the table. Cardinal Richelieu, whose principle of *raison d'état* applied to the Catholic Church as well as the Huguenots, was confronted with the fact that France's entire land border was ringed by Habsburg troops, thanks to the Spanish occupation of the western half of the lower Palatinate. This was not good for France, and the best way to break this stranglehold was to support the Protestant cause in the empire. Richelieu couldn't do this openly, however, since he was not willing to risk war with Spain, plus he didn't want Protestant armies moving across France. So he decided to bankroll the Protestant side secretly, with Denmark as the front man for the effort.

There is no need here to go into all the ins and outs of all the campaigns in the war. Suffice it to say that the Danes invaded the empire but were consistently beaten by imperial forces under the overall command of the brilliant but enigmatic Count Albrecht von Wallenstein. Wallenstein was a Protestant who had fought on the imperial side in the Bohemian phase of the war and was made duke of Friedland in 1623 in recognition of his military, diplomatic, and administrative services. Tilly was continuing the war in the south against Saxony, but Maximilian of Bavaria feared the Protestant alliance would target him and so appealed to the emperor for help. Ferdinand hesitated because of the potential cost, but Wallenstein, convinced by astrology that he was destined for greatness, offered to raise the army himself. Ferdinand agreed, and made him overall commander of the imperial army. Wallenstein converted his estates into virtual factories for producing war material and supplies, and thus was able to boost his own territory's economy while developing a remarkably efficient system of logistics to supply his armies—which he supplemented with extortion from the towns of friends and foes alike. Tilly and Wallenstein (who generally ignored imperial orders and went his own way) defeated the Protestant armies, and in 1629 Christian IV of Denmark was forced to sue for peace, renouncing his claims to bishoprics and territories south of Schleswig and Holstein and agreeing not to interfere with imperial affairs.

Enter the Swedes

In the wake of this victory, Ferdinand decided that the time had come to roll back Protestantism and set the stage for its complete abolition within the empire. In the Edict of Restitution (1629), Ferdinand decreed that all ecclesiastical territory that had fallen into Protestant hands since 1552 be restored to Catholicism and that Calvinism be banned. Since the two remaining Protestant electors had both absorbed a number of ecclesiastical lands, and one of them, the elector of Brandenburg, was a Calvinist, this would have effectively crushed the Protestant side altogether. Ferdinand overreached himself, however; the victory and the follow-up made the Habsburgs far too powerful, so that even the Catholic powers of Europe lined up to oppose them. Maximilian of Bavaria led a coalition of princes in an effort to check imperial power, France accelerated its efforts to undermine Spain, and even Pope Urban VIII began looking for ways to prevent Spain from increasing its power in Italy. At the same time, the Habsburgs suffered some unexpected setbacks even as they were cleaning up in the empire. After the expiration of the Twelve Years' Truce in 1621, Spain immediately declared war on the Dutch. After some initial success in the southernmost portions of the Dutch Republic, they failed to follow through, perhaps waiting for the war in the empire to run its course. The Dutch felt no such compulsion, however. They took the war to the sea, and by 1627 had driven Spain into bankruptcy; the following year, they captured the entire Spanish New World treasure fleet. Spain was clearly in trouble. In part to take pressure off Spain, imperial forces had conquered and occupied most of the southern coast of the Baltic, from Danzig (Gdansk)—the main port used by the Dutch in the lucrative grain trade, the foundation of the Dutch economy—to Lübeck. This brought a new power into the conflict: Sweden, under its young and energetic king, Gustavus Adolphus.

Gustavus had been involved in a war with Poland (as well as with Christian IV of Denmark) over control of the Baltic. Although motivated by his strong Lutheran faith, Gustavus was reluctant to get into a war with Ferdinand until after he had secured Sweden's position by defeating Denmark and negotiating a peace settlement with Poland (with the help of Richelieu). Ferdinand's expansion into the Baltic posed an immediate threat to Gustavus, however, and so he decided to go on the offensive. Gustavus was a genuine military genius. He introduced a number of important innovations on the battlefield, particularly a tremendous expansion of field artillery together with an unprecedented degree of coordination between infantry, cavalry, and artillery. He was thus a match for the Catholic generals, who had pretty much had their own way up to this point.

Gustavus landed in Pomerania in June 1630 with a small but well trained and experienced force of 13,000 men. The Protestant princes were reluctant at first to accept his help; they believed the cause was hopeless, and even if Gustavus could help, they did not want to risk Swedish domination. Gustavus told them he wasn't interested in the empire; he just wanted to protect Swedish interests in the Baltic. The Protestants were unimpressed. But the Catholics were not prepared to deal with him either, largely because Ferdinand had fired Wallenstein. Wallenstein had wanted to turn the empire into an absolutist state similar to France, and to do this, he argued that the Edict of Restitution was a mistake and that a balance of power between Catholics and Protestants would better serve the empire and Habsburg power by eliminating an intractable and divisive issue from the political equation. Catholic states, and particularly Bavaria, rejected both the goal of absolutism and Habsburg hegemony, and the means to reach it. Conservative forces thus pressured Ferdinand to dismiss Wallenstein right after Gustavus's forces had landed. Tilly was given command of the imperial army and had to spend some time reorganizing it. Gustavus thus had a six-month period where he could secure the Baltic ports, prepare his troops, and negotiate financial support from France.

Even still, the Protestant side dithered about supporting the Swedes until 1631, when the city of Magdeburg—an early ally of Gustavus—fell to imperial forces under Tilly. The city was plundered and burned, and 75 percent of its inhabitants slaughtered. The Protestant side realized that that would be their fate unless they could stop the imperial armies, so they sent troops to Gustavus's side. In September, the combined Protestant forces won a decisive defeat over Tilly and the imperial army at Breitenfeld, north of Leipzig. This was followed by a series of victories that saw Prague fall into Saxon hands, Gustavus enter Munich, and Swedish forces plunder Bavaria.

A number of the more colorful stories of the Thirty Years' War come out of this period. Two of the best known involve the Lutheran cities of Rothenburg-ob-der-Tauber and Dinkelsbuhl. In 1631, Tilly stormed Rothenburg and planned to level it. To try to win his good will, the town council gave Tilly a three-liter tankard of its finest wine. Tilly, being somewhat chivalrous in outlook, told the councilors that if they could find someone who could drain the tankard in one swig, he wouldn't raze the town. (Might we have here the origin of 7-Eleven's "Big Gulp"?) A retired mayor named Nusch said he'd give it a shot. He managed to finish it, then fell asleep for three days. But Tilly was good to his word and spared the city. Despite being overrun with tourists, it is today one of the most picturesque towns in Germany, with its medieval walls largely intact.

Dinkelsbuhl, though Lutheran, had its brush with disaster with another Lutheran, one Gustavus Adolphus. The town had been forced to supply food for several armies in the area when Gustavus's forces arrived and asked for bread. The citizens, sick and tired of being constantly shaken down, told Gustavus to take a hike—not the brightest thing to do, considering that Gustavus had the Swedish army and its cannons with him. So Gustavus decided to destroy the city, Lutheran or not. The children of Dinkelsbuhl, however, didn't want to see their town flattened, so they collected all the food they could find and brought it out to Gustavus. Gustavus was impressed with their action (and besides, he got his food), so he spared the city. To this

day, Dinkelsbuhl holds an annual festival celebrating the children saving the town.

My personal favorite story is the taking of Würzburg castle by the Swedes. Würzburg was owned by a Catholic prince-bishop, and when the Swedish army approached the city, he skipped town and left the defense of the castle in the hands of an inexperienced lieutenant. The lieutenant wasn't going to let the Swedes attack the castle without a fight, so he lined his men up outside the gates, planning to have them fire one volley and then cross the drawbridge into the castle, pull up the bridge, and lock the doors behind them. Unfortunately, the Swedish advance was so quick that the soldiers panicked and ran inside without firing, and with the Swedes on their heels they took the drawbridge before it could be raised. But they still needed to get past the outer doors then through the inner doors in order to take the castle. The lieutenant thought that his initial plan didn't go well, but he knew the Swedes would have to break through the outer doors to attack him, so he loaded a cannon and pointed it at them, intending to fire it when the Swedes broke through, wheel it through the inner doors, and lock up again. This was basically the same plan he had for the outer defenses, and you'd think he'd have learned from his mistake. The Swedes had some Scottish engineers with them; as one might expect, they were a bit crazy, so they asked Gustavus if they could run up to the doors, hang a bomb on them, and blow them down rather than mess around with a battering ram. Gustavus agreed, and the ensuing explosion so panicked the Würzburg troops that they left the cannon loaded and pointing at the gate and ran inside. The Swedes came in, turned the cannon around, blew open the inner gates, and took the castle.

In the midst of the Swedish advance early in 1632, Tilly

was killed in battle outside of Munich. This forced Ferdinand to recall Wallenstein, who had been toying with joining Gustavus. Wallenstein agreed to return, on condition that the Edict of Restitution be revoked. Ferdinand agreed, and Wallenstein took command again. He drove the Saxons out of Bohemia, but was forced out of winter camp into battle at Lützen in November 1632. The Protestants defeated the imperial army, but Gustavus was killed in battle. Protestant reverses followed, but Wallenstein was again dismissed in 1634, this time for negotiating on his own with Sweden, France, and the Protestants for a peace settlement. To make this dismissal stick, Wallenstein was then assassinated. In November 1634, imperial forces defeated the Protestants at Nördlingen.

The early 1630s thus demonstrated that the imperial forces could not hold the northern parts of the empire and that the Protestants could not hold the south. In May 1635, with the Peace of Prague, the internal conflict in the empire was ostensibly settled; ecclesiastical lands were returned to those who held them in 1627 (prior to the Edict of Restitution), pending a final decision to be made jointly by Catholic and Protestant judges, and a number of territories changed hands. All leagues and armies were to be disbanded with the exception of the imperial army, which was to be used to keep the peace.

The Spanish Phase

This wasn't the end of hostilities, however—after all, it was only the seventeenth year of the Thirty Years' War. After Nördlingen, Spain was preparing a full-scale attack on France, so in November 1634, Richelieu made a deal with Sweden, Baden, Hesse-Kassel, and Würtemberg (the Heilbronn Alliance) to attack the Spanish Netherlands.

Richelieu then made an alliance with Savoy, Mantua, and Parma to make good France's centuries-old claim to Milan. So in May 1635, just as the Peace of Prague was being signed, Richelieu declared war on Spain, without incurring so much as a protest from Pope Urban VIII. About a year later, the emperor declared war on France, and Germany once again became a battleground, though this time the war also extended well beyond its borders. By 1639, Spain was once again in trouble. The Dutch destroyed most of the Spanish Atlantic fleet, and in 1640 Catalonia and Portugal revolted against the crown, with Portugal regaining its independence. The last Spanish invasion of France was turned back in 1643, the year Louis XIII of France died.

The Peace of Westphalia

France and Sweden, who had been denied territorial concessions in the Peace of Prague, won numerous victories but could not enforce their demands by military force. Meanwhile, the princes of the empire wanted peace as well, and so in the early 1640s negotiations began to try to settle matters. There was so much bad blood between the principals that they refused to sit down together, relying instead on messengers to carry proposals and counterproposals back and forth. Given the speed of travel, it is perhaps no surprise that a peace settlement didn't really begin to fall into place until 1648. The process began with Spain throwing in the towel and recognizing the independence of the Netherlands in March. This broke the logjam; Sweden declared a cessation of hostilities within the empire in August in Osnabrück, Westphalia, as did France in September in Münster, also in Westphalia. Finally, the Peace of Westphalia was signed in Münster in October, ending the war within the empire. (Spain and France continued to fight until 1659, and Sweden, Poland, and Brandenburg until 1660, but those conflicts need not concern us here.)

The Peace of Westphalia had to settle both religious and political questions. On the religious front, it reaffirmed the Religious Peace of Augsburg, but added Calvinism into the mix as an acceptable religion. Religious boundaries were reset to where they were on January 1, 1624, and princes were allowed to change their religion but not to confiscate the property of those exiled for religious reasons. Religious minorities that had been in place in 1624 were to be tolerated. Politically, Sweden was given Western Pomerania, confirming its control of the Baltic and enabling it to emerge as a major power in Europe. Brandenburg was given Eastern Pomerania, along with several bishoprics. Bavaria got the Upper Palatinate and the electoral office, though the Lower Palatinate was restored to its legitimate ruler, who was given a new, eighth electoral vote. This had the effect of strengthening Catholic Bavaria and Protestant Brandenburg, both of which could then act as a counterbalance to the emperor, who no longer played a major role in German affairs even as an arbitrator. For their part, the Habsburgs were given control of Bohemia and Hungary along with their hereditary property in Austria, effectively creating the Austrian Empire. France was given Metz, Toul, Verdun, Pinerol, and the imperial territories in Alsace except for Strasbourg, thus preventing Habsburg encirclement. And all sides acknowledged the independence of the Netherlands.

The losers of the war were the people of Germany. Almost every territory within the empire lost at least 40 percent of its population during the course of the war. The huge gunpowder armies foraging (i.e., plundering) across the land stripped it bare of crops and livestock and condemned the region to over a century of recurring famine—despite the fact that in 1600, Germany was able to produce enough grain to feed its population. Plague also raged during the period; Augsburg lost 18,000 people to the disease in the 1530s. The economic devastation combined with high levels of personal and governmental debt led to rampant inflation as well. It is no wonder that even after two world wars, the people of Germany to this day remember the Thirty Years' War as the most devastating the country has ever seen.

The Thirty Years' War marks the ending of the period of the Reformation, at least on the Continent. It combines in itself many of the trends of the "long" sixteenth century (1450–1648): religious conflicts between Catholics and Protestants and, in some cases, Protestants and Protestants; complex relationships between religion and politics; dynastic rivalries between the Habsburgs and the kings of France; the tension between early modern absolutism and the further development of medieval constitutionalism and limitations on central power; and the rise of the Dutch and the

decline of Spain. It also marks the end of the medieval papacy as a major political force in Europe and signals the shift of power in Europe away from Germany—which was too devastated to play a major role in the late seventeenth and early eighteenth centuries—and toward France and Great Britain. Most significantly, however, it was the last of the wars of religion on continental Europe. The Reformation had run its course; the Latin West was now permanently divided into multiple competing camps, and while hostility between them didn't go away, at least they were no longer killing each other over which were true followers of the Prince of Peace.

There were ongoing problems, of course, notably the persecution of Protestants in France, culminating in the Revocation of the Edict of Nantes in 1685, not to mention the English Civil War and its aftermath, but for the most part religious questions ceased to be major issues in the internal politics of at least the continental European states. The exhaustion over religious warfare, the effects of the Renaissance, the implications of the discovery of the New World, the scientific revolution, the recovery of ancient skeptical writings, all combined to create a new ethos and mindset in Europe, leading ultimately to the Enlightenment and the development of modern science.

But that's another book entirely.

Questions for Discussion:

1. The Thirty Years' War was a very complex and messy affair. What elements do you think were the most important to the war (religion, dynastic politics, differing political philosophies, etc.)?

2. How do you account for the massive devastation of central Europe caused by the Thirty Years' War? Along

with the economic consequences, what psychological effects do you think would have accompanied the destruction? How might this have shaped attitudes in the second half of the 1600s and into the 1700s?

3. Can you think of any modern examples of political, ethnic, national, and personal rivalries that have erupted into wars? Does the tangle of motives and causes of the Thirty Years' War offer any insights into these modern situations?

Bibliography

Augustijn, Cornelis. *Erasmus: His Life, Works, and Influence.* Trans. J. C. Grayson. Erasmus Studies 10. Toronto: University of Toronto Press, 1991.

Cottret, Bernard. *Calvin: A Biography.* Trans. M. Wallace McDonald. Grand Rapids: Wm. B. Eerdmans Publishing Co., 2000.

Dickens, A. G. *The English Reformation.* 2nd ed. University Park, PA: Pennsylvania State University Press, 1991. Contrast to Scarisbrick's revisionist account.

Duke, Alastair. *Reformation and Revolt in the Low Countries.* London: Hambledon Press, 2003.

Elwood, Christopher. *The Body Broken: The Calvinist Doctrine of the Eucharist and the Symbolization of Power in Sixteenth-Century France.* New York: Oxford University Press, 1999. More technical, but excellent analysis of the pivotal issue in the French Reformation.

Gordon, Bruce. *The Swiss Reformation.* Manchester: University of Manchester Press, 2002.

Holt, Mack P. *The French Wars of Religion, 1562–1629.* New Approaches to European History. Cambridge: Cambridge University Press, 1995.

Kingdon, Robert M. *Adultery and Divorce in Calvin's Geneva.* Cambridge, Mass.: Harvard University Press, 1994. Provides an example of the impact of Calvin's reforms on daily life.

Kittelson, James M. *Luther the Reformer.* Minneapolis: Fortress Press, 2003.

Lindberg, Carter. *The European Reformations.* Oxford: Blackwell, 1996.

Bibliography

MacCulloch, Diarmaid. *The Reformation: A History*. New York: Viking Books, 2004. The best current survey of the Reformation.

Mattingly, Garrett. *The Armada*. 1959. Reprint, Boston: Houghton-Mifflin, 1987. A detailed account and a great read.

Mullett, Michael A. *The Catholic Reformation*. London: Routledge, 1999.

Nauert, Charles G., Jr. *Humanism and the Culture of Renaissance Europe*. New Approaches to European History. Cambridge: Cambridge University Press, 1995.

O'Malley, John W. *The First Jesuits*. Cambridge, Mass.: Harvard University Press, 1993.

Parker, Geoffrey, ed. *The Thirty Years' War*. 2nd ed. London: Routledge, 1997.

Pettegree, Andrew, Alastair Duke, and Gillian Lewis, eds. *Calvinism in Europe 1540–1620*. Cambridge: Cambridge University Press, 1994.

Scarisbrick, J. J. *The Reformation and the English People*. Oxford: Blackwell, 1984. A "revisionist" history, in contrast to Dickens.

Sproul, R. C. *The Holiness of God*. Wheaton, IL: Tyndale House, 1985.

Steinmetz, David. *Calvin in Context*. New York: Oxford University Press, 1995.

———. *Luther in Context*. 2nd ed. Grand Rapids: Baker Academic, 2002.

Tracy, James D. *Europe's Reformations, 1450–1650*. Lanham, MD: Rowman & Littlefield, 1999.

Williams, George Huntston. *The Radical Reformation*. 3rd ed. Kirksville, MO: Truman State University Press, 2000.

Index

Index

238

Index

Index

Index

Index